How do I teach
…and keep my sanity?

Kathy Paterson

Pembroke Publishers Limited

© 2002 Pembroke Publishers
538 Hood Road
Markham, Ontario, Canada L3R 3K9
www.pembrokepublishers.com

Distributed in the U.S. by Stenhouse Publishers
477 Congress Street
Portland, ME 04101
www.stenhouse.com

We acknowledge the financial support of the Government of Canada through the Book Publishing Industry Development Program (BPIDP) for our publishing activities.

National Library of Canada Cataloguing in Publication

Paterson, Kathleen M., 1943–
    How do I teach? ... and keep my sanity / Kathy Paterson.

Includes bibliographical references and index.
ISBN 1-55138-149-4

1. Teaching.   I. Title.

LB3013.P38 2002   371.3   C2002-902792-6

Editor: Kate Revington
Cover Design: John Zehethofer
Typesetting: Jay Tee Graphics

Printed and bound in Canada
9 8 7 6 5 4 3 2 1

Contents

Introduction:
Making the Moments Matter

Teaching is all about the relationship between teacher and student—about the wonderful bond that not only makes learning happen, but encourages the development of the whole child and empowers the child to become an independent, lifelong learner and contributing, confident member of society. This fostering is the goal of every teacher, but unfortunately, it can become lost in the melée of other daily demands of the profession.

There is always so much to do. Time is the teacher's most precious commodity, and most fearsome foe. Rudyard Kipling once wrote, "If you can fill the unforgiving minute, with sixty seconds worth of distance run …" If you could do that, you'd be a teacher who is efficiently using time, but you'd probably still feel like you are so far behind that you're first. Time is the teacher's albatross. When there is not enough of it to go around, it can interfere with the cherishing of the children—the most important facet of teaching—as well as the respecting of personal needs, desires, and health. Too often I have heard excellent teachers say that what with everything they had to do, they felt like they were verging on nervous breakdowns. Teaching is a tough job. But it is possible, I believe, to be an outstanding teacher and keep your sanity too.

Every teacher wants to use time efficiently not only to cover the extensive curriculum, but also to foster every student's personal growth and development. In order to do this effectively, teachers need to be authors, who stimulate imagination; artists, who captivate attention; and actors, who hold that attention until the final word is spoken. They also need to be wizards, magicians, and guiding angels. But above all, teachers are nurturers. They want to spend *quality* time encouraging, caring for, and supporting their students; they don't want to watch time being frittered away in meaningless pursuits.

Have you ever had a vision of having time to spend, one on one, with each of your students on a regular basis? How often have you said, "There aren't enough hours in the day to …?" or, " I didn't even have a moment to speak to … today!" Teachers want their students to feel important and special. Every teacher dreams of being able to squeeze a few extra moments into each day for quality time with students. It becomes increasingly difficult to do this, though, when changing curriculums, extracurricular activities, record keeping, reporting, professional development, and so on are constantly demanding more teacher time.

It is possible to make those extra moments and to collect them into precious minutes for student nurturing and guidance. As you do this, you can alleviate some of the pressure felt from always being behind. It is also possible to use in-class time so wisely that all, or at least most, of the students will be on-task, focused, and productive. In this book, I share some ideas that will address these issues. Sometimes, even simple suggestions can save both minutes and sanity.

Teachers want to find time to build a class with lots of spirit, accountability, and personal ownership for success. Such a class exemplifies learning and uses time well. However, in the day-to-day reality of teaching, there is never enough time to compile lists of good ideas for hooking students into a lesson, to read all the available literature on how to get and maintain attention effectively, to create motivational beginnings for all lessons, to stay on top of the ever-changing curriculum, and still be able to sit patiently and listen to a child's problems, direct his questions, explore his interests, and celebrate his successes. When a teacher is rushed for time, listening to an individual student is often the first thing to go. Or, perhaps, when one-on-one time is finally available, the teacher's individual tutoring, listening, and advising skills may be less than honed.

This book presents you with some useful lists that will help you achieve your professional goals. It features inventories of ideas for effective use of class time, for motivating activities, and for efficient ways of relating to students and dealing with common classroom problems. You will find ways in which you can save a few moments each day to add to the "student bank"—the time spent on teaching students and being there for them.

All of the suggestions proposed here have been tested in the classroom. Many will probably be familiar to you already. Some ideas may not be completely original, but all are useful, and all will help you to deal with the chaos that often accompanies teaching. They will allow you to maximize the minutes with your students. For, when dealing with students, *you* have the whole world in your hands!

1

Communicating with Students Well

Teachers talk to students. That's what they do best. That's what they love to do. That's how they create a positive learning environment and build rapport with their students, making every moment spent in quality talk time paramount to effective teaching. Consequently, the more minutes saved throughout the day, the greater the chance of quality teacher/student conversations. The next step, of course, is to make every one of these precious minutes count.

Teachers often talk more to young people than any other adults do. I always get a chuckle out of the "teachery" jokes that reflect this point. For example: "Teachers are the ones who give their mates 'either/or' statements" or "Teachers are the ones who say to the mechanic who failed to fix the car, 'Are you *sure* you gave this your best effort?'" When teachers talk, students listen.

You know that precious one-on-one time spent talking with your students can foster their personal growth and self-esteem, can often prevent potential problems, and can aid in the learning experience. Individual time given to students is, perhaps, the most nurturing aspect of any teacher's day. It is up to you to make that time, then use it wisely. You need to talk to your students daily, in small groups, in large groups, in pairs, and individually. I will never forget the articulate Grade 3'er who wisely informed me that her teacher was "the best" because she "always talked about important stuff," or the young man in Grade 11 who, on a questionnaire about what made a teacher memorable, responded, "The teacher I will remember for the rest of my life was Mr. ___. He always had time to listen, no matter how busy he was. He would put down what he was doing and really listen. We had some of the best talks that year. I think we all learned more from those talks than from anything else." Everyone needs to talk; quality talk time with students is what makes teaching authentic and meaningful.

Today, perhaps more than at any other time in history, discussion is important. As a teacher, you need to know how, when, and where to open the door to discussion and how to lead that discussion effectively. Naturally, there are obvious moments for conversation all day long, during the actual lessons, for example; however, there are other valuable ways of incorporating discussion into your daily plans, too; in so doing, you will be promoting positive self-concepts, attitudes, and work habits, as well as fostering classroom respect and cohesiveness. That is what teaching is all about!

This chapter focuses on communication. It begins with suggestions for talking to students on an everyday basis as well as in crisis situations. As a teacher, you have experience talking with your students, but even after many years in the profession, I have sometimes fumbled for words, or wondered just how to talk to a particular child. The following lists feature strategies that I have found worked successfully for others and me.

The act of one-on-one tutoring, direct communication to teach or reinforce skills, cannot be overlooked. It is, perhaps, the original form of individual talk time. In this situation, a single student is given full attention. The trick for effective tutoring lies in knowing just how to make the most of the brief time allotted. The steps suggested in this chapter should help.

As every teacher knows, it is usually the same student who is tutored repeatedly; it is common knowledge that *all* students deserve equal attention. Therefore, tips on ways in which to ensure that *every* student gets some one-on-one talk time with the teacher are valuable too.

Similarly, the whole-class "grand conversation," or discussion, is another familiar form of talk. Although all teachers use tutoring and grand conversations regularly, other techniques can be used in the classroom to tap into the power of conversation. These include silent talk, walk-and-talk, response cards, the help spot, meet 'n' greet, and the power punch, as well as the group establishment of class rules and the use of class meetings and sharing circles—a wonderful idea borrowed from our Aboriginal neighbors. All of these strategies are based on open conversation and discussion. All are forms of communication that help to build rapport, strong self-concepts, and class unity. All make for a smoother running, more unified, more functional classroom where little time is wasted and learning is enhanced. Just what the teacher ordered!

General Tips for Talking to Children

We all think that we can talk to children easily, but sometimes even the best teachers are lost for words. Having specific ideas as a reference has helped me in the past.

- Create an open environment.
Children need to know that they can talk to you freely, without fear of consequences. Be open, friendly, concerned, and ready to listen. Let them know it's OK to talk about anything in your presence.

- Initiate the conversation.
Getting the conversation started is often the most difficult part of talking to children. Follow their lead if they begin talking, but be ready with gentle suggestions or open-ended questions in case they are silent.

- Find out what they know.
Children often don't reveal much information on their own. Ask direct questions about the topic under discussion to ascertain exactly what the students do and do not know already. You will gain valuable information for leading the conversation.

- Listen carefully with your heart.
Children need to feel that you are totally there for them. Carefully listening to children helps to build their self-esteem. They realize you care. In addition, listening with your eyes as well as your ears may give insights into unspoken feelings.

- Don't rush children.
Sometimes, it takes children a long time to say exactly what they want to say. Avoid paraphrasing too quickly or finishing every sentence.

- Communicate your own ideas.
Children want to know what you think. Be prepared to share thoughts, feelings, and similar personal situations. Doing so will give children confidence in your responses.

- Talk to children in their own language.
Children like to hear their own vernacular in use. Depending on the age of the student, certain vocabulary is appropriate or inappropriate. Using the common terms, phrases, and idioms of the age group will make the conversation more meaningful.

- Be honest about what you know.
If you don't know an answer, just say so, but then suggest that you will "find out."

- Be supportive and positive.
In one-on-one discussions, don't be judgmental. Rather, support children's ideas, direct them if necessary, and be sure that the talk ends positively.

- Suggest a course of action.
Children want answers, or solutions, even if it's just to agree to talk again tomorrow.

The Road Less Travelled: Talking to Children About Disaster

By disasters, I mean more than worldwide disasters, but also the many daily crises with which children must deal. These include family separations or deaths, deaths of pets, illnesses, and monetary concerns, to name just a few. Life is difficult for children, more so every day. It is important to know how to talk to them about adversity.

1. Clarify facts with compassion.

   Find out what children know as well as what they want to know. Make a professional judgment as to how much they *need* to know. Sometimes, less is better, but, depending on the age of the student, honest information is important. For example, telling a six- or seven-year-old alarming details of a situation would be foolish. On the other hand, a ten- or eleven-year-old may demand details. In the latter case, honesty, without unnecessary elaboration, is the best policy.

2. Realize that children probably know more than they will initially admit to.

   Children are often reticent to talk. In any crisis, whether personal or global, they frequently know more facts than you might want them to. They hear and see many versions of the same issue. Remember this when talking to them. What they believe may be far from the truth, but it is based on their reality and must be dealt with carefully.

3. Acknowledge their fears.

   Children need to know it's OK to be afraid. Accept their fears. Suggest that you, too, have concerns and that being frightened is normal and acceptable.

4. Answer questions honestly.

   Children need to trust in you. Answer their questions as honestly as possible, keeping in mind that a simple honest answer is better than loading them with unnecessary facts and details.

5. Offer realistic reassurance.

   Children in crisis need a tender hand. Tell them that you and other adults care for them and about them. Let them know that they are safe.

6. Don't preach.

   Children need simple talk. Don't moralize or discuss right and wrong. Stick to the facts and concerns at hand, and deal with them directly. For example, in the case of a family crisis, such as a separation, no judgments should be made. Instead hold an accepting, compassionate, and honest talk about what has happened and how the child can deal with it.

7. Be empathetic; share your feelings.

   Children need to know that you care and have feelings about the issue too. Tell them how you feel about the situation. Doing so allows them to view their own emotions more openly and realize that they are acceptable and normal.

8. Accept any inappropriate responses, and deal with them later.
   Children don't always behave as expected. Some will react to disaster with humor or foolishness. Recognize that these are coping strategies, and make a note to talk to these children one-on-one at a later date.

9. Address common fears gently.
   Even if specific common fears, such as the fear of being separated from one's family, are not expressed, use your professional judgment to recognize them and talk about them.

10. Always suggest coping strategies.
    Children need concrete solutions. Tell them what works for you. "I was really upset too, so I went for a long walk … talked to my friend … drew a picture … wrote a long letter to …" Then brainstorm for possible strategies, some of which can be carried out in the classroom.

Finding Ways to Have Talk Time for All

It's easier to find time to talk to some students than to others. The following are suggestions for making sure that every student in your class gets some personal teacher talk time. Not all methods will work for everyone; choose the one or two that appeal to you.

- Individual Talk Time by Invitation

Pick a time (first five minutes of lunch, recess, or after school) when students are invited, on a rotational basis, to come and talk with you about whatever. Some students may choose not to take advantage of this offer; others will be thrilled. Give each your full attention for five minutes. In my experience, once a student has experienced Talk Time by Invitation, he can hardly wait for the next. Topic? Whatever the student chooses.

- Walk-and-Talk

Turn the invitation talk time into walk-and-talk by going for a walk with the student at the prescheduled time and chatting as you walk. Doing so removes the possible discomfort of having to sit facing a grown-up to talk. The brisk, brief walk can be outside around the school, in the gym, or wherever. The added advantage here is the shared exercise.

- The Homework Call Makeover

Call students at home to remind them of a particular project, assignment, or test that is coming up or due. They love the attention, plus the few minutes taken to make the call may save many minutes of following up undone work later.

- The Power Punch

During the year, visit as many students as possible at some activity *outside of school*. For example, attend a dance or piano rehearsal or a community league soccer game. (An in-school extracurricular event such as a drama production works too, but not with quite the same punch.) Students who have been "visited" will be filled with importance. They can't believe that their teacher would care this much. Your pay-off is that they will then work harder in class.

Keeping in Touch by Note and Deed

- Silent Talk
  Children treasure positive remarks. Giving students little notes to take home, again on a rotational basis (use your register to keep a checklist so as not to miss anyone), is an excellent form of communication. Notes should be short, simple, and positive. A note per student once a month works well and demands little time. It takes about one minute to write a note and because of the increase in self-worth for students, it is time well spent.

- Casual Response Cards
  Children like writing and receiving notes. Small index cards made readily available to students can serve as excellent two-way communication mediums. Students write their questions/concerns in point form and put cards in a box on your desk. You respond directly on the card and return it as soon as possible. Shy students particularly love this technique, and the small size of the cards removes the intimidation of a whole, blank page.

- Formal Response Cards
  Children enjoy communicating with you privately. Set aside five or ten minutes once a week for students to fill in small response cards, just as they might in the previous technique. Over the weekend, you briefly respond to each student. Students love this way of receiving personal communication from the teacher, and sometimes valuable information can be gleaned from their comments.

- The Help Spot
  Even *model* students need help sometimes. Arrange for a special area, for example, a table or desk near the back of the room, and officially name it the Help Spot. On a weekly rotational basis, call students to the Help Spot during a time when the class is working. The student can bring a problem, curriculum related or otherwise. Teach students to respect each other's time at the Help Spot and not interrupt or expect teacher assistance at this time. A sign "Help Spot in Use" will remind them of this. If a student has no problem, discuss strengths.

- The Tutoring Table (*see "Cruising Through Tutoring," page 18*)
  Children like to choose when they want help. When students are working, teachers usually circulate to provide individual help. An effective alternative is to sit at a specific place, the Tutoring Table, where students come to you for assistance. Your presence at the tutoring table means an automatic, open invitation for students to seek help. In addition, students tend to try a little harder on their own before seeking assistance. Rules such as "no more than three students at a time" can be established if desired.

- Meet 'n' Greet
  Children love being acknowledged. Stand at the door, daily, first thing in the morning, and personally greet each student as he or she arrives. Try to make comments as personal as possible. ("Mary, how is your new baby brother? Johnny, I like your new backpack.")

It's OK to Talk: Helping the Silent Sentinel in Class

A few students in every class never seem to speak. They are easy to overlook, and they need teacher intervention to encourage their inclusion in class discussions. Sometimes, the quieter students just need more teacher attention in turning the discussion towards them. Others, however, pose a more difficult problem. The following pieces of advice have worked well for me with *some* of these students. With others, I had to admit defeat and allow them their silence.

- Talk together.
  Invite the student to have a mini-conference with you. Express your concern and ask why the student doesn't take part in discussions. If the problem can be identified, deal with it. If not, try another approach.

- Tip off students about upcoming topics.
  Before a big discussion, let quiet students know what the topic is so that they can "practise" a couple of good responses ahead of time. Sometimes, this awareness is enough to take the edge off any fear of speaking. Then make a point of asking these students for a response.

- Coach students on how to begin talking.
  Show students possible ways to begin expressing a thought. Something as simple as learning a few phrases, such as "I think" or "In my opinion," can make a difference to the student who doesn't know how to begin.

- Ask students whether they agree with comments already made.
  When a student is reluctant to express any idea, he may be more ready to agree with an idea already expressed, and even to add *why* he agrees. By specifically asking the student whether he agrees with a comment, you give him a chance to add positively to the discussion.

- Teach good discussion practices to all.
  All students need to be taught the rules of a discussion, from not monopolizing the conversation to taking turns, to deliberately trying to involve someone else. Praise students for good techniques such as carefully listening to each other.

- Invite quieter students to speak.
  It's easy to get caught up with the "talkers." Invite the more quiet students for their input. Discourage talkers from taking over by politely saying, "I'm glad you have so many ideas, but I'd like to hear from …"

- Control the discussion.
  You can closely monitor how many times students speak during a discussion by limiting the number of times they speak. Explain that for this one discussion you want to ensure that everyone has equal opportunity; therefore, each student can speak only twice, for

example. Not only does this encourage the quiet students, but it makes the talkers think twice before they speak and choose their thoughts more carefully.

- Establish a signal.
  You can manage the problem of runaway conversation between the talkers, which prevents the quieter students from getting a word in edgewise, by establishing a "pause" cue, the raising of your hand, for example. On this cue, all will be silent, allowing you the opportunity to directly ask a quiet student for input.

- Set "quiet-kid" goals.
  During a mini-conference with a quiet student, challenge the student to speak one time only during the next discussion (or day, or half day, or class … whatever). Offer praise when he accomplishes this, then up the ante. Using this "baby steps" technique, the quiet student will gain confidence to talk more.

Note: Remember that not all children are blessed with linguistic intelligence, and as a teacher, you should recognize this and respect their wish to remain silent if that is what they decide. There are many other ways in which they can demonstrate their skills and understanding.

Cruising Through Tutoring: General Tips for Tutoring One-on-One

Of course you know how to tutor. You're a teacher! However, in my own experience I found that often when I sat with a student to tutor one-on-one, I didn't know where to begin. The following list is a set of sequenced steps that work well for tutoring. The first four steps should take no more than about four minutes.

1. Greet first.
   Make the student feel comfortable (she knows she's there because of a problem) by saying a few words unrelated to the area of difficulty. "You did a great job in gym today when you hit that home run."

2. Ask the student what the problem is.
   The student's assessment may be different from what you see. If she doesn't know, continue with step three.

3. Determine the difficulty.
   Through a series of questions, as well as a quick scan of the student's work, try to figure out the main area of concern.

4. Begin the session with something that the student *can* do.

5. Model an example of what the student is required to do, while the student observes.

6. Take two steps forward, one step back.
   Break the task into small components and teach/review the first step. Once step one has been mastered, add step two. Stop. Review steps one and two together before adding step three. Stop. Review from step one again, and so on. Be positive and supportive. Expect mistakes and use them as your guide to how to reteach the concept.

7. Coach.
   Instead of giving the student "answers," prompt or cue so that she comes up with the correct responses or strategies herself. Give partial answers if necessary.

8. Reinforce correct moves or answers constantly.
   Tell the student what she has done correctly.

9. Remember back-pocket strategies.
   Always have a Plan B, an alternative way of teaching a concept, and a Plan C and D if necessary. All students can learn. We have to find the right way to teach them.

10. End on a high.
    Always end a tutoring session on a positive note. Point out advances made, even if the whole concept or problem has not been solved. Leave the student with the belief that she can succeed in this area.

Creating Working Rules

Every classroom needs to have good rules that are easy to follow and reinforce. This special kind of communication will reduce inappropriate behaviors, off-task time and, consequently, teacher intervention time. If all the students "buy into" the rules, they will be more successful. Here is a sequence of steps for establishing and promoting class rules.

1. Discuss the need for class rules.

2. Brainstorm for possible rules. (Students will usually think of many.)

3. Complete the worksheet titled *Thinking of Class Rules*. Older children will write responses, beginning with the completion of individual worksheets. Then responses are compared with those of one other class member and five possibilities are selected. Next, each pair of students shares their five possible rules with one other pair, and the new group of four students settles on three possible rules which they then present to the class. Younger children brainstorm all possibilities and the group leader will scribe these.

4. Accept all the groups' rules, then paraphrase them, developing a few rules that seem to encompass most of the students' ideas. Discuss your paraphrased renditions of their rules to see if they still cover everything and fit students' expectations. With younger children, decide together which rules are most appropriate.

5. Limit further to three or four *generalized* rules. Suggested rules: (1) Be on time; (2) be prepared; and (3) respect yourself and others.

6. Review the finished rules and discuss what each involves. What specific behaviors does each imply? Be positive. Don't suggest what the rules do *not* imply or what behaviors would *break* the rules.

7. Arrange to have the rules posted in an attractive, colorful manner. You might choose students to create the poster.

8. Reinforce adherence to the rules daily by specifically referring to them. For example: "Steven did a good job of not getting involved in that argument. He was following Rule 3 on respect."

9. Review the rules once a week. Here's a "fun" way to do so. "Close your eyes and tell me what Rule 2 is," or, "If I decide to share my lunch with Gina, which rule would I be following?" Keep the review positive. Don't say, "Which rule would I be breaking if …?"

10. Make parents aware of your class rules through newsletters or class meetings.

Thinking of Class Rules: Student Worksheet

Classroom rules should promote a comfortable environment. Think of five to ten rules that you think should be enforced in your classroom so that students and staff can get their work done.

Consider such things as

- space
- noise
- property
- work

- atmosphere
- likes and dislikes
- personal space
- visibility of blackboard, overhead, etc.

Individual

1. _____
2. _____
3. _____
4. _____
5. _____
6. _____
7. _____
8. _____
9. _____
10. _____

Partners (Pair up with someone and combine your ideas into five rules.)

1. _____
2. _____
3. _____
4. _____
5. _____

Groups (Get together with another pair; combine your ideas into three rules.)

1. _____
2. _____
3. _____

Making an Offer They Can't Refuse: The Class Meeting

Students love class meetings. The fact that they have a say in what happens in the class empowers them, provides them with some degree of ownership over their own education, and aids in the development of a sense of "togetherness" in the classroom. Honest expression of thoughts, ideas, and opinions is encouraged, as students become involved in problem solving. In addition to being a terrific way to resolve conflicts, make decisions, and develop personal self-concepts, the class meeting provides an authentic learning experience. The following steps will take you through the form of the class meeting that has worked well for teachers I know.

1. Teach a mini-lesson on the characteristics and uses of a meeting.
   Compare a class meeting to the typical "town meeting" or any type meeting with which the students will be familiar. Teach the sequence of events in a meeting: the call to order, a review of what happened in the previous meeting, an agreement on the reason for the new meeting, discussion on the topic, reaching of a consensus or making of resolutions, meeting summary, and close.

2. Teaching "I" is the way to go.
   Teach students how to use "I" statements. Explain how use of an "I" statement, for example, "Sometimes **I** don't like it when …" avoids offending or angering others. It is especially effective when expressing emotions. Practise the use of "I" statements by creating a hypothetical situation of conflict, such as two opposing views on where the class should go for a field trip. Have students work in partners. Each partner adopts a different position, and they argue, using "I" statements. It may be necessary for you to model first. Select a pair who exhibit good use of "I" statements to demonstrate for the class.

3. Discuss "Just Us Justice."
   Discuss how the class is responsible for its own justice within the meeting. Pre-established classroom rules should be enforced here, as well as the one-person-speaks-at-a-time rule.

4. Agree on a consistent time and place for meetings.
   Doing so adds importance to the gathering. Possible meeting locations outside the classroom might include the library, a room normally used for adult meetings, an empty art or drama room, or even a stage if the school has one. Monthly meetings work well for most classes, given their hectic schedules. Allow at least an hour for each meeting.

5. Establish an issues book.
   This book for ideas can be a simple scribbler in which students can write problems, note issues, or make suggestions for the agenda at the next meeting. It should be readily available in the same spot so students can record ideas before possibly forgetting them. Issues such as where to go on a field trip or how to decorate the room are easily handled in the class meeting.

6. Appoint the big wigs.

   Discuss the roles of meeting leaders (president, vice-president, secretary, and treasurer). With older grades, students, on a rotational basis, may lead the meetings, but with primary, you should be the "president." Having different students take turns at being the "secretary" is a good idea: many skills are learned and practised. It is useful to have two students work together at this job. Have them "read the minutes" at the following meeting.

7. Remain true to form.

   Conduct meetings as close to the correct format as possible. Encourage all students to "have a voice," realizing that some students will choose to keep quiet.

8. Reserve one part of the meeting for teacher concerns.

   At this point you can raise any concerns you have and invite discussion about them.

9. Close with confidence.

   Children remember the last thing they hear. Be sure that you close the meeting, so that you can summarize the main findings, issues, and decisions. Sometimes, you may have to use your authority to resolve problematic issues. Sometimes, the resolution may be to "shelve the issue" until the next meeting.

10. Make the most of minutes.

    A valuable after-the-meeting activity is to have students summarize, in writing or pictures, the events of the meeting. This activity not only incorporates the cross-curricular idea, but serves as closure.

Developing the Sharing Circle

Similar to the class meeting, but based entirely on the Aboriginal Natural Laws of love, honesty, sharing, and determination, the Sharing Circle promotes cohesiveness, airs concerns, and offers support to all. It is a beautiful concept of togetherness, truly exemplifying the gentle spirit of our Aboriginal neighbors. The purpose of a Sharing Circle is more to deal with emotional concerns and facilitate group assistance to individuals than to deal with more practical problems. I suggest that both class meetings and Sharing Circles be used in a classroom, with the Sharing Circle being more on an as-needed basis. The following are the natural steps for conducting a Sharing Circle.

1. Introduce the concept of Aboriginal Natural Laws.
   Teach the laws of love, honesty, sharing, and determination (strength), as well as the purposes and format of the Sharing Circle. Review these laws before each session.

   Note: Native peoples believe that by following the Natural Laws an individual will remain "grounded" and at peace.

2. Discuss the inherent strength of a circle.
   A circle can't be easily broken, has no sides, and has edges equidistant from the mid-point. Chairs will be set in a circle to show strength in the group plus equal voice for all.

3. Establish the rules of a Sharing Circle.
   Rules should be as follows.
   - Only one person speaks at a time.
   - Everyone is given equal respect and careful attention.
   - Conversation moves around the circle in a clockwise manner.
   - What each person says is considered important.

4. Let students sit where they want.
   Allow students to sit randomly in the circle; assure them that all are equal and united in it.

5. Choose the topic of discussion.
   For the first few times, select the issue to be discussed. Issues should be pertinent to all or most of the students, until they become more familiar with the Sharing Circle and more open to discuss issues that involve only a few of the members. Possible initial issues could include concern about upcoming tests, problems with peer relationships, and problems with parents' expectations.

6. Invite a student to begin speaking.
   Introduce the topic and *invite* someone to begin. Once a student has accepted the invitation and spoken, others follow in sequence. If no one volunteers to begin, you should take the initiative.

7. Respect the right to remain silent.

   Any student may choose to "pass" rather than speak. Usually after the first few Sharing Circles, students seldom pass and feel eager to share their thoughts.

8. Let the circle be unbroken.

   Generally no one should interject thoughts, suggestions, or ideas until everyone has had a chance to speak in an orderly fashion. Encourage students to listen carefully to everyone's words, and to practise empathy and compassion.

9. Review what was said.

   Since you have the leadership role, summarize the ideas presented, or ask others to comment further on what has been said. Individuals may make compassionate suggestions to others or to the group as a whole.

10. Show mutual appreciation.

   The Sharing Circle is then closed with a joining of hands and a moment of silence to show appreciation for peers, as well as for any spiritual guidance received. Native peoples end with a prayer. School groups could end with a quiet song or silent thought.

2

Building Rapport and
Class Spirit to Last

Good rapport with students, like positive class spirit, doesn't just happen. Both have to be cultivated tenderly and nourished consistently. Once established, rapport and class spirit create a class where minimum time is wasted and students feel a sense of commitment and belonging. I believe the time invested in establishing and maintaining rapport is never lost. The class functions smoothly!

You want to be able to use your precious time in the classroom, the minutes you have consciously saved through the diligent use of streamlined strategies and techniques, to effectively present curriculum, teach skills, and foster the personal development of every child. And, as you probably know, the first step towards achieving this goal lies in the development of a positive rapport with the students. If students are willing to work with you, if they are eager to please you and, if they like you and have genuine respect for you, rapport has been established and with it, a constructive learning environment. Ask any student when and why he experienced his most successful school year. He will tell you the grade and add that it was because he really liked his teacher. Along with that goes the understanding that his teacher really liked him, as did at least *most* of his peers.

It is necessary, therefore, to take the time early in the year to launch your program for creating positive rapport, as well as class spirit, then to continue to foster them both throughout the year. Just because you have created the bonds initially doesn't mean they will remain. Like any relationships between humans, they need constant maintenance and proactive measures; *maintenance* measures, such as the ones discussed in this chapter, will, in the long run, save valuable time that might otherwise be spent on such pursuits as disciplining.

The process begins with getting to know your students, while at the same time letting them learn about you. Then throughout the year you need to demonstrate to your students that you really care. Your students need to know you like them. Naturally, it's not possible to like every student equally, but as a professional, you must give all equal respect, compassion, and energy.

Perhaps the first step is to realize that children, unlike adults, have short attention spans, are naturally restless, and may not want to be at school, or, at least, confined to a desk. The Medicine Wheel of Aboriginal peoples reminds us that schools should take more than the mental aspect into account. This wheel is divided into four equal parts, showing the four necessary components of life: *physical*, *mental*, *emotional*, and *spiritual*. All of these components must be in balance if a person is to function to the best of his or her abilities.

The teacher who exercises sincere concern and compassion for her students will automatically incorporate activities from the physical, emotional, and spiritual quadrants of the

Medicine Wheel, as well as the mental. In so doing she will be taking the whole child, as opposed to the "academic child" only, into consideration.

The Aboriginal Medicine Wheel

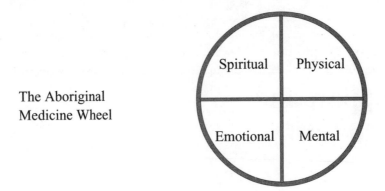

What are these activities? Activities from the spiritual, physical, and emotional quadrants are frequently the ones that strengthen and sustain student-teacher rapport, as well as class spirit. But how can you establish and maintain this positive balance without taking away time from the curriculum? This chapter deals with some of these issues.

There are many ways to create positive relationships. One way is to follow some of the one-on-one strategies suggested in Chapter 1. Another is to plan activities that demonstrate your understanding of the students' needs, wants, likes, and dislikes—activities that encompass all four parts of the Medicine Wheel. These include exciting ways to turn students on to a particular lesson, to refocus wandering attention in interesting ways rather than by yelling or nagging, to make students feel that the classroom belongs to them by creating walls that work, to quickly regain flagging rapport, and to generally make students feel special.

Finally, this chapter addresses the difficult problem of year-end good-byes to children with whom you have developed powerful, positive rapport and who feel a sense of camaraderie and ownership for the class. It's not as hard as it sounds!

Getting Off to a Strong Start: Tips for Establishing Rapport

Good rapport begins the moment that students walk into your classroom. It doesn't just happen automatically, though. In addition to having a positive attitude and wearing a smile, consider acting upon any of these ideas that have worked for many.

- Make your students feel wanted.
  In the week before the school year begins, take a few minutes to phone all the students in your class and welcome them to your room. The time spent is well worth the strides made in establishing rapport later.

- I know your name.
  Children want you to remember their names. Use each student's name as frequently as possible. For example, when handing back a paper, say "Here's yours, Jane," or "Thank you, Corey." Play a couple of name games. For example, you might learn as many names as possible, then have students switch desks and see how well you can remember. Children love to see that you are trying to learn their names and also understand that you are human and make mistakes.

- Smile. You're on candid camera.
  Children want you to know who they are. On the first day of school, have students make colorful name tags (or have them already made for young students). Let them get into small groups (less threatening than on their own) and pose in any manner they wish for photographs. Develop the pictures quickly, and you can have all their names learned by the next day. Meet them at the door day two, and greet them by name. Use the pictures later for "class captions." (See page 30.)

- Here's looking at you, kids …
  Children need to know you care! Start by letting them know you like them, feel excited and privileged to be their teacher, and are there for them for the entire year. Really look at them while you talk.

- Welcome to the room.
  Children love treats. Fill a brown paper bag with tiny treats (for example, erasers, candies, pencils, and pencil sharpeners) and allow each student to pick a welcome-to-our-room prize.

- Share and share alike.
  Your students want to know about you. Prepare a talk about yourself, including details on hobbies, funny anecdotes, humorous calamities … whatever you think may interest them. Share this and then ask students to share something of themselves. Don't make the sharing mandatory this early in the year, though; accept some students' need to "pass."

More Tips for Establishing Rapport

Establishing rapport is such an important part of effective teaching that here are more good ideas to consider.

- Two heads are better than one.
  Children often like talking about other children more than about themselves. Let students get into pairs. Use your professional judgment about whether to allow free choice or to tell them to turn to the person behind them. Ask students to find out something interesting about their partners, then share this with the rest of the class.

- T-charts reveal likes and dislikes.
  Children enjoy expressing their likes and dislikes. Display a T-chart that illustrates *your* personal likes and dislikes that do *not* have to do with school. Depending on student age, your chart can be on an overhead, on a poster board, in words, or in pictures. For example, under the Like column, you might have *chocolate ice cream, rainbows,* and *butterflies.* Under the Dislike column you might have *toothaches, asparagus,* and *cold weather.* The students instantly learn something about you; they can then create their own T-charts.

- Show students you're human and ask for help.
  Every teacher has a few foibles in the classroom. Early in the year, share a few of yours, and actively solicit students' help. For example: "I have trouble keeping my desk tidy and I need you to help me with this by not putting your work here." "I sometimes don't hear you if your voice is tiny; I need you to be patient and speak a little louder." Admitting such problems doesn't make you appear weak or less of a teacher; it shows that you respect the students' ability to help.

- Finish that thought.
  Children enjoy simple sharing games, such as completing open-ended sentences with whatever comes to mind. Go around the room doing this and keep the sentences simple. You begin all the sentences; students repeat the stem, then add the endings. The same stem can be used several times in succession for fun comparisons, or even with the entire class. Not only does this create an atmosphere of sharing and amusement in the classroom, but it may even provide you with initial insights about your students. Here are a few examples:
  - My favorite color/animal/food/game is
  - When I go home today I will
  - I like/hate/care about/wonder about

- Fill a Fun Box.
  Students cherish their Fun Box, a box filled with an assortment of comics, easy readers, magazines (especially at Junior High level), mazes, coloring books (especially the new design and fantasy ones), joke books, decks of cards, and puzzles. The Fun Box is a must in every classroom. Students quickly learn that when they have completed their work, they may select something from this box. Ask students what they want to see in the Fun Box. Getting their input encourages a sense of ownership.

Fun Box: Student Worksheet

Check the items you would like to see in the box. Rank your five favorites, with 1 being your most favorite.

❑   1. comics

        Suggest names _____

❑   2. joke books

❑   3. maze books

❑   4. coloring pages

❑   5. colored markers

❑   6. drawing paper

❑   7. deck of cards

❑   8. magazines

        Suggest names _____

❑   9. small hand-held games

❑ 10. puzzles

❑ 11. word searches

❑ 12. other suggestions _____

Would you be willing to contribute any items to our Fun Box? If so, what?

_____

_____

What restrictions do you think should apply to use of the Fun Box?

_____

_____

Working Walls That Improve Class Spirit

Creating a classroom where students feel welcome does much towards establishing and maintaining positive rapport, and it can all begin with the walls. Aside from the many wonderful and thought-provoking posters that have flooded the market, and, consequently, classrooms, there are other ways to fashion a hospitable and functional classroom. The following ideas, as well as promoting rapport, also work towards the saving of time, either by their easy design or functionality.

- Create a Graffiti Wall.
Children love writing on walls, and if there's paper, for example, brown wrapping or colored paper, they can do it. Cover a section of wall and have flow pens available. Invite students to write or draw anything they want here, with the exception of put downs or profanity. Assign the regular replacement of the paper to the students.

- Feature your cast of stars.
Students of all ages love to see their names in print. Before the term begins, make and display one or more of the following:
  - students' names printed inside cutouts of leaves, snowflakes, flowers, CDs, cartoons, traced profiles, traced hands, or whatever, and mounted on the wall
  - a huge birthday chart (a circle divided into 12 pie slices works well) indicating when each student has a birthday
  - a big, colorful list titled "Members of Our Class"
  - a People chart: beside each student's name, note his or her pet peeve, favorite color, favorite TV show, etc. As you get to know your students, you can add these details.

- Fly your own flag.
Children love to display their pride. Creating a class flag or banner is a great way to instill class pride and develop rapport. Brainstorm for ideas. Let the class pick the artists. A student worksheet for creating the flag appears on page 34.

- Create class captions for candid photos.
Take candid photos of your class (as well as using the "name" pictures taken day one), and affix humorous thought bubbles (available where film is sold) to the snaps. You can have the photos enlarged to full-page size with a color photocopier. Pictures can be arranged to form a collage or "crazy quilt," with appropriate headings. Students of all ages love to look at these over and over again.

- Let students wish on a wall.
Students are attracted to the idea of making suggestions that may affect their classroom. An interesting twist on the familiar Suggestion Box is the Wish Wall. Decorate a section of wall with a fanciful poster or picture or even just the words "Wish Wall," attach an oversized envelope, decorated by an artistic student if possible, and pin a stack of small pieces of paper or index cards beside it. Encourage students to place suggestions (wishes) in the bag at any time. You can divert a lot of "complaining" by this easy technique. Simply say, " Put it in the Wish envelope."

Practical Items to Post

Students spend a great deal of time in your room, so it is important to surround them with valuable visuals and information. Here are other ideas for effective use of the classroom walls and bulletin boards.

- Say bye-bye to news blues: Post what's happening.
Class news, happenings in the school, important dates to remember, changes to schedules … Children invariably forget times, places, and dates. To deal with this issue create a News Board and post all information. Assign a student to keep the board updated, then refer students to it for answers.

- Post tips for muddled minds.
Help forgetful children out. Post frequently needed rules, as for spelling and math, on a designated section of a wall. Chart paper and dark flow pens quickly create this wall, where students can rapidly access important information without bothering you. Near exam time, post tips for studying as well as an exam schedule.

- Create bills of rights.
Students misbehave, and sometimes class rules aren't enough. Display both the Students' Bill of Rights, and the Teacher's Bill of Rights on one section of wall. Make creating the bills a class project, and be sure to keep them simple and short. Review the bills often as a proactive, time-saving measure. Bills posted visibly on one wall can be quickly referred to if a problem or issue arises. In one instance, a substitute teacher constantly had to interrupt her lesson in order to discipline a few students until another student quietly pointed to the Bill of Rights. The Bill clearly stated *Respect for all.* A quick reading of the Bill provided the substitute with the power she needed to better manage the misbehavers.

   The student worksheet that follows can be copied and used for student input. Tallying the results will provide a total group consensus of the five to ten most valued rights for each Bill of Rights. Explain that, although you want students' input as to which of the listed points they consider the most important, the final decision on the Teacher's Bill of Rights will be yours.

Classroom Bill of Rights: Student Worksheet

Below is a checklist of possible rights that you may want to have in the classroom. Check the five (or more) points that are most important to you. Next, number those points in order of importance, with 1 being most important. Feel free to add other points if necessary. "Teacher" refers to your home-room teacher.

Student Rights

❏ Right to my own space (my desk) _____

❏ Right to be allowed to sit wherever I want to _____

❏ Right to expect fair treatment from my teacher (no "pets") _____

❏ Right to feel safe (not picked on) in my class _____

❏ Right to expect the class to be quiet when we are working _____

❏ Right not to be embarrassed by teacher or peers _____

❏ Right to chew gum in class _____

❏ Right to be called on to speak when my hand is up _____

❏ Right not to be forced to speak when I don't want to _____

❏ Right to be treated with respect by the teacher _____

❏ Right to be treated with respect by my peers _____

❏ Right to go to the washroom when I need to _____

❏ Right to move around the room when I want to _____

❏ Right to ask for help and not feel badly doing so _____

❏ Right to expect teachers to be prepared for lessons _____

❏ Right to expect work to be marked as soon as possible _____

❏ Right to be given a passing grade in all subjects _____

❏ Right to know my grade level during the year _____

❏ Right to expect honesty from my teacher _____

❏ Right to be treated according to my age (not like a baby) _____

❏ Any others? _____

Classroom Bill of Rights: Student Worksheet

Now, check off rights that you believe the teacher should have in the classroom. Number those rights in order of importance, with 1 being most important.

Teacher Rights

❑ Right to expect students to listen when I talk _____

❑ Right to expect students to be prepared for class _____

❑ Right to expect students to show respect for teacher and peers _____

❑ Right to expect students to help each other with work in class _____

❑ Right to expect students to do their best work _____

❑ Right to expect students to leave items on my desk alone _____

❑ Right to expect homework done on time _____

❑ Right to expect honesty from students _____

❑ Right to expect students to be quiet at all times _____

❑ Right to expect students to not chew gum or eat in class _____

❑ Right to expect students to get enough sleep at nights _____

❑ Right to expect students to be polite _____

❑ Any others? _____

A Classroom Flag: Student Worksheet

Think of ideas for creating a flag or banner that will tell others about our class. Use this worksheet to help you plan.

1. What symbols or pictures should we use? _____

2. What text should we have on the flag or banner? _____

3. What type of lettering should we use? For example, bubble letters, capital letters, script, or lowercase letters? _____

4. What three colors do you think would be the most effective? _____

5. Should we have a white or colored background? _____

6. Should we make a flag or a banner? _____

7. What size should we make the flag or banner? _____

8. Who do you think should be responsible for the drawing, the coloring, and the lettering? _____

9. Where should we display our finished product? _____

10. What would you like to do to help produce the flag or banner? _____

_____

_____

Rationale for Refocusing Activities

Students become distracted, unfocused, even chaotic at times. Once rapport is established, one of the quickest ways to lose it is to overreact to this loss of focus: to shout, nag, or whine about the situation. The lesson may have bombed, the students may be tired, or it may simply be too close to Christmas (or Halloween, or March Break).

At these times you realize that you have lost the class temporarily and must somehow bring it back. You need to introduce simple activities that will allow the students to get rid of some of their excess energy in a constructive, teacher-led manner. They will then return to work more easily. Such activities tap into the physical and emotional quadrants of the Medicine Wheel. They demonstrate an empathetic understanding of the nature of the whole child. When using them, however, it is important to remember the following points.

Terms of Reference

• You, as the teacher, remain in control by explaining that students will all have a five-minute break, then will return to work.

• Directions and expectations (especially for returning to work) are clear.

• The "risk" factor is very low, since students remain in their desks and are working or competing only with one other person. Even shy students enjoy these activities.

• Students learn from social interactions and from games. These activities, then, are not time-wasters, but rather, time savers. Time is not lost in nagging children to return to work.

• These activities are organized, mini–learning situations that also provide for the parts of the child not normally addressed in the academic curriculum.

• By using one of these activities to refocus a class, you are *strengthening,* rather than weakening, your positive rapport with the students.

Five-Minute Refocusing Activities

These are the refocusing activities, together with brief explanations of each. Sometimes, you can choose a few students to "show off" for the whole class at the end of the class activity.

Verbal Activities

• Word Pong
In this exercise in quick talking, students in partners or trios rapidly toss single words back and forth between them, keeping to a teacher-provided theme. The first student to stammer or say "uh" is out. Possible themes include colors, food, games, famous people, occupations, and objects whose names begin with a certain letter. Older students enjoy a word association version of the same game.

• Fortunately/Unfortunately
During this verbal exchange, partners discuss a topic, alternately starting each sentence with "fortunately" or "unfortunately." One partner is A; the other is B. You provide the first line, for example, "Fortunately, I did my homework."

• No Repeats Please
This playing-with-words verbal activity requires partners to discuss a topic using different words to say the same thing. You provide the starting phrase, for example, "Look at the sky." Partner A repeats the phrase, B says it differently, A finds another way to express it, and so on. Thus "Touch your nose" could become "Hold your nail on your nose."

• Free Talk
Students are given precisely one minute (or more) to take part in a conversation and *must* do so. As soon as you announce "Stop!" all talking should cease.

• I Know What You Mean
Students conduct an imaginative conversation in which they discuss an unknown topic. Once the teacher provides the first line, for example, "They are big and scary," partner A mentally decides what it refers to and repeats it with feeling. Partner B interprets the line too, without sharing the meaning, and adds another line, for example, "And they smell bad too." They continue adding to the story, eventually sharing what they were thinking about.

• Pass a Hug
As the teacher, you begin this whole-class activity. You might say, "I pass a hug to Erin because I know she is working hard to improve her writing." Students tell each other what they appreciate or like about their peers through verbal rather than physical expression. Encourage them to be specific in their comments and to choose peers who haven't already been chosen.

• Alphabet Anyone?

Students engage in a creative, quick-thinking, often foolish conversation in partners or trios. They discuss a topic, starting each phrase or sentence with the next letter of the alphabet in sequence. Example: **A**n apple is on my desk. **B**ut it is not a very good apple. **C**an I have yours then?

• Bad-a-Boom

In this whole-class counting activity, each student in sequence must say either a number or the phrase "bad-a-boom." "Bad-a-boom" is said whenever the number 5 would come up. For example, 25 is "2 bad-a-boom." For older students, you could have two number substitutions or substitute for all multiples of that number; if 5 is "bad-a-boom," then 10 would become "2 bad-a-boom."

Physical Activities

• Thumb Wars

In this physical coordination exercise, partners wiggle their thumbs in an attempt to control their opponents' thumbs. They try to force their partners' thumbs down.

• Silent Scream

Through physical behavior only, students demonstrate various emotions to partners. You provide the cues: cheer, cry, laugh, be terrified, think, be worried, and so on.

• Number Targets

Partners open closed fists simultaneously, holding out any number of fingers they choose, in an attempt to jointly reach a particular number that is called out. Increase the difficulty by having trios aim for a larger number.

Quick Refresher List for Slipping Spirits

Sometimes, you know in your heart that things aren't going well, and that, just perhaps, the positive rapport you worked so hard to establish—the good feelings you don't want anyone to forget—are in jeopardy. Given the importance of maintaining good classroom rapport, here is a list—a refresher list, if you will—that may help you stop the downhill slide and pick up endangered spirits.

• Smile—and mean it.

• Dare to be different.
Children love the unexpected. Stop the "usual" for the moment and be spontaneous—play a game, take the class for a walk, or turn all the desks to the back.

• Ask the experts.
Children like to offer advice. Ask them what should be done to make things better in the classroom or to improve class atmosphere. They will tell you.

• Obtain success secrets from "rich and famous" peers.
Tell a colleague that you are having "difficulty with the class," and ask for advice. You will receive helpful hints, or at least, empathetic shoulders.

• Rate your enthusiasm.
Waning enthusiasm or energy for teaching can have disastrous effects on rapport. See if yours needs a tune-up; if it does, put things in perspective and get going!

• Get your funny bone tickled.
If your sense of humor is in remission, rapport will suffer. Challenge your students to tickle your funny bone. They will, and flagging rapport will get a shot in the arm.

• "Do lunch" with the kids.
Students respond positively to personal out-of-class attention. Invite small groups of them to accompany you for lunch, either in or out of the school. Or, take an in-class coffee break, where you supply the drinks and cookies.

• Let students make choices.
Offering choices about what to do when will not only enhance rapport, but will develop independent thinking and problem-solving abilities.

• Appreciate your true treasures.
Take a few moments to tell each member of the class one thing that you appreciate about him or her. Praising students does wonders for rapport and promotes their self-esteem.

• On your mark, get set—slow down.
Taking a few minutes to be truly approachable, to sit quietly, to maintain eye contact, and to listen to your students may be all that you need.

Finishing with Flare: It's So Hard to Say Good-bye

It is your professional obligation to make the year-end transition as smooth as you made the beginning of the year. The positive rapport that you have firmly established and maintained with your students can pose a problem when it comes to saying good-bye. As you know, the end of the year can be traumatic for everyone. You may seldom or never see many of these students again. They know this, and the idea of losing someone to whom they have become attached can be distressing. For all, the end of the year is a bittersweet time, but you can make it easier.

• Create a forum for feelings.
Children need to express fears of separation. A couple of weeks before the last day, bring up the topic of saying good-bye and encourage discussion. Share your feelings, too.

• Be the class crier. Help your students to remember the "good stuff."
Towards the end of the year, begin each day with a Remember When session, where you remind them of interesting or fun activities, as well as content areas covered during the year.

• Keep tricks up your sleeve till the end.
Your students don't want the last days to drag anymore than you do. Be prepared with exciting activities and lessons right up until the end. (See Chapter 4 for suggestions.)

• Write bread-and-butter letters.
Children love to express appreciation. Have them write thank-you notes to the secretaries, assistants, custodians, principal, and volunteers for all their help during the year. Doing this helps the students to experience a sense of closure.

• Conduct a Merry Maid class.
Students need to experience closure visually. Sometime in the last week, involve all of them in a general class clean-up, where the walls are stripped, shelves emptied, and so on. It is fun to provide each student with a paper apron, signifying the Merry Maids. This clearing-the-room action helps them to realize that the year really has come to an end.

• Find the *well* in Fare*well*.
Encourage your students to think positively. Discuss all the good things in the year ending. Talk about new opportunities, teachers, friends, and skills, as well as the completion of activities that students might not have liked so much.

• Loosen those ties that bind.
Some children are terrified of leaving their teacher. Close to the end of the year, gently begin the moving-away-from-them process. Hold discussions about independence, reinforce independent actions, and talk about your faith in them.

Good Ways to End the Last Day

The last day is frequently one of hurried farewells, hasty hustling of students on their way, and general confusion. Students remember beginnings and endings. It is your responsibility to make their final day with you as memorable as their first. Here are some ideas that may help.

• Say it again.
Students are intrigued by simple phrases said in different languages. In the last month of school, challenge them to find as many ways to say "good-bye" as possible, such as *Au revoir* (French), *Dasvedanya* (Russian) etc. Make a chart of the new words, and encourage their use on the last day. Doing this helps to lighten up the act of saying good-bye.

• Bestow thanks.
Children never tire of hearing "good stuff." Purchase little packs of thank-you cards and write quick notes to all of your students, thanking each of them for something specific. For example: *Thank you for being so helpful ... creative ... mature.*

Give these notes out on the last day. They will not only provide a final self-esteem boost to your students, but a little closure for you, too.

• Speak now, or forever wish you had.
Children want to know how you feel about them, especially now that they have invested a year of their short lives with you. Prepare a little speech, telling them what you gained from your year with them. Be positive. Let them know that it was a growing experience for you, too. Both you and your students will gain a sense of closure.

• Be ready for bye-bye blues.
Students get attached to you. No matter how much you think you have prepared them, some will suffer separation anxiety on the last day. Be ready to show gentle compassion, but at the same time, effect closure for them by firmly saying good-bye.

• Be your own breath of fresh air.
Allow yourself a few moments to reflect on your personal successes during the year. You will probably be exhausted and ready for the break, but don't overlook the importance of closure for you, too. End the year on a positive note. You have made a difference in many lives.

3

Dealing with Challenges in Peer Relationships: Group Work and Bullying

Part of being an educator is helping children to learn to work and play together. Your challenge is to integrate all of them into a cohesive, smoothly functioning group in which they can practise the social skills necessary for successful adulthood.

Besides monitoring how your students interact, you can incorporate strategies that will directly influence and reinforce peer relationships. One such technique is group work. Many teachers shy away from group work because, if not handled correctly, it can be chaotic and less than profitable for many of the students. But group work is important. Teachers who believe in authentic teaching let students work in groups, at least some of the time, for life is about cooperative functioning with others.

However, a pet peeve with students (and often with parents) is the manner in which groups are formed. Letting students choose their own groups always results in the same students being together, sometimes with disastrous consequences. It is, therefore, important to let them know, early in the year, that all groups will be flexible, that is, changed frequently, and will be formed by you. There are two considerations here:
• grouping for cooperative learning
• random grouping
The former is for authentic, curriculum-related work groups, whereas the latter is more for fun activities. Points will be made about the formation of each.

With all this focus on group work, it becomes necessary to justify, especially to the more intelligent and/or conscientious students and their parents, its merits. How often have you heard, "Why should I get the same mark as ___ when I did all the work?" or, "I don't want to work in a group because some kids do more work than others." A list of good reasons for group work, where groupings are teacher chosen and heterogeneous, has been included.

Sometimes, however, problems do occur and children can be cruel and thoughtless. Such is the case with the bully. Numerous detailed books, seminars, and full-length courses are available on handling bullying. My intention in this chapter is to provide readily accessible, hands-on lists for teachers and students, for immediate use when confronting the issue. The ideas presented here include suggestions for instant teacher intervention, specific hints for the children who have been bullied, and suggestions for a whole-school program.

Finally, this chapter includes tips for making and keeping friends, for the basis of every smoothly functioning class or small working group is positive peer relationships.

Points to Ponder on Cooperative Learning Groups

- Cooperative groups are created by you for specific learning opportunities: They are flexible and exist for one project only.

- Ensure that group members have different ability and skill levels.
  Unlike the homogeneous groups frequently used for such activities as reading, cooperative groups are heterogeneous.

- Pre-choose the roles (leader, recorder, researchers, collectors, presenter, interviewer, artist, editor), being sure that all students get a chance to take each role during the year.

- Encourage group members as they learn to rely on one another: everyone is important and interdependent.

- Encourage face-to-face interaction—it is not only necessary, but desirable.

- Give each group its own place to work.
  Consider offering the back corner of the room, the hall outside the door, a spare room, or part of the library. Plan this ahead of time.

- Look for strong individual accountability.
  Each individual has a role within the group, as well as a final, independent role, such as writing a review of what was learned or doing an assignment based on the knowledge and skills required.

- Expect to see interpersonal skills and problem-solving skills practised and refined.

- Have students evaluate both their group and themselves.
  The evaluations, which can be written or oral, should take place after students complete the project, performance, or presentation.

- Give each student a separate score based on functioning within the group, as well as a final, individual written or oral evaluation of the actual learning.

- As the teacher, be sure to plan carefully for group combinations, group roles, exact directions and expectations, places for each group to work, and evaluation criteria.

Justifying Those Groups

There are many good reasons, other than because working with others can be fun, for including group work in the school program.

- Working in groups simulates real life.
We have to work and live with others, and the results are not always fair. Getting experiences with this in school prepares students for reality.

- Problem-solving behaviors are learned.
Groups naturally experience problems; they learn to deal with them, and solve them together. The teacher provides guidance, but the students actually solve the problems.

- Social skills are practised.
It is impossible to work in a group and not refine social skills. Students encounter a variety of different personality types and must learn to deal with them appropriately. Once again, this situation mirrors real life.

- Friendships can be made.
Often, after working together in a group, students who might otherwise have nothing to do with each other form new friendships. Group work is an excellent way to introduce students to varied types of people.

- Self-confidence is addressed.
Although some children enter the group situation with nothing but confidence, many do not. However, because they are assigned specific roles within the group, all students experience a sense of achievement. Peer pressure makes sure of this, at least in most cases. Confidence is given a boost.

- Peer tutoring is implicit.
A natural development is that the stronger group members often find themselves "tutoring" the weaker ones. The stronger learn tolerance and have an opportunity to refine skills; the weaker learn new strategies and skills.

- Commitment is inherent.
All members of a group feel a sense of commitment, even if some do not express it. They want their group to be successful and at the same time do not want to "pull the group down." They want to do their part and may be more responsible than if only looking after their own interests.

- Learning can include failure.
Sometimes, working in a group can be difficult for everyone, and the resulting achievement may not be what was expected or desired. In this case, group members can be helped to see where they had trouble and why they got the mark they did. This then becomes a learning situation for everyone and, once again, it simulates life, where we are often constrained in our efforts by others with whom we must work.

Random Groups: Nine Fun Ways to Create Groups for Fun Activities

- Adding Two and Two

  Students turn to their neighbors and carry out some part of the upcoming activity, for example, brainstorming. Pairs join other pairs to continue the activity. Eventually, students can join to make groups of eight if necessary. Each time the group gets bigger, concessions and agreements must be made.

- Making Fast Families

  This method requires some teacher preparation. A container of names is passed around. On a cue, students have to find the other members of their "families," either by making appropriate noises or miming only. Each family consists of Father, Mother, Child, Grandmother … (depending on how many persons are needed per group). The first family together and sitting on the floor wins. Students love this activity which takes less than five minutes.

  Possible families:

  By mime

  Wiggle family, Soldier family, Itchy family, Sneezy family, Dizzy family, Cranky family, Smily family, Wooden leg family

  By sound

  Any animal group, Wind family, Thunder family, Cymbal family, Engine family

- Finding Similarities in Words

  Prepare words, groups of which are, in some way, similar. For example, choose colors, words ending in *ing* or *ed*, or words starting with the same letter. The words chosen can reflect any recent study, for example, words from a Language Arts story or words from a Science unit on electricity. Groups can form based on words that are exactly the same (eg., 5 "copper wires") or words that relate to each other in some way (eg., characteristics of the protagonist in the story). Follow the same routine as for Fast Families, except that, on cue, students mingle and discuss their words until they find a match.

  Note: Younger students can be told what the similarities are. Older students can find these out themselves as they mingle.

- Matching by Color

  For this fastest and simplest way to group a class randomly, pass a container of colored chips or colored squares of paper. Use Tidley winks or prepare laminated sheets of different colors, cut into one inch squares. The chips can be reused many times. People with the same color form a group.

- Building Compound Words

  Prepare small slips of paper with parts of compound words on them, for example,

  | mail | flower | sun | box | shine | shoe |

As you can see, there are several possible combinations, *mailbox* or *shoebox, sunflower* or *sunshine*. On a cue, students must find someone with whom they can build a compound word. This activity creates partners. Any students who cannot find a match are paired off at the end and called "mismatches." To create groups of four, partners must find other pairs such that the two compound words can be used within a sentence. Example: The *sunflower* was put in the *shoebox*.

• Counting Handshakes

Either go to each student and whisper a number based on how many groups are desired *or* hand out tokens with numbers on them. The first option allows you to "stack" the groups however you want them to be mixed up, since you know to whom you have whispered each number. With the second option, laminated number tokens can be kept for future use. On a cue, students get up and begin shaking hands with each other. The number of "shakes" each person gives to another depends on his particular assigned number. For example, a student given the number "3" pumps hands three times. It quickly becomes obvious who has another "3" as that person will stop shaking at the same time.

• Finding Commonalities

Draw your students' attention to the fact that many of them have things in common that they are not even aware of. Start by having students write their middle names on small slips of paper (I always keep a container of cut-up paper pieces on my desk for instant use); then, instruct them to find others whose middle name begins with the same letter. Since you will probably end up with unequal groups, group further by using such cues as people with the same number of letters or same second or last letter in their middle names.

• Mimicking Animals Soundlessly

Pass out papers with the names of animals on them. Students, on cue, must find the others with the same animal names on their papers, but they must do so silently. Some animal choices that work well are monkeys, elephants, and eagles.

• Talking the Talk, Walking the Walk

Slips of paper containing simple directions for both movement and speech are passed out. On cue, students must find other group members by doing what is written on the paper. For example, a student with a paper saying "Soldier: Yes, sir!" would march stiffly around and say, "Yes, sir" to every student he meets. Other suggestions include "Dancer: Dance with me"; "Singer: Let me entertain you"; "Athlete: I'm number one"; "Old timer: Oh, my aching bones"; "Teacher: Be quiet, class"; "Dentist: This won't hurt a bit"; and "Lawyer: I object." The number of identical slips depends on desired group size.

Confronting Bullying

Many schools exercise zero tolerance for bullying, but the individual teacher is still frequently the first one who must deal with a bullying situation. Schoolyard bullying is the negative result of a power differential between students, with the bullies being both aggressive and impulsive in nature, often as a result of witnessing aggression at home. One misconception is that bullies are actually timid and scared, hiding behind their bully masks. This is seldom the case; more frequently, they have antagonistic, angry personalities and are, therefore, difficult to re-educate.

The following condensed sequence of tips has helped me to interact effectively and consistently, at least initially, with the parties in a bullying incident.

1. Verify the facts.
    Since the teacher is seldom a first-hand witness in a bullying situation, it is necessary to find out exactly what happened from as many sources as possible, including the students directly involved. Always encourage the reporting of bullying!

2. Make quick jot notes of the incident.
    When, in your professional judgment, the facts are clear, quickly jot down a few notes about time, place, incident, and so on. (You will finalize these later.)

3. Next, talk to the child who has been bullied.
    The child will be in need of your support and compassion. Validate the child's feelings and show trust and caring. Reassure him that you take the problem seriously and will be involved in its solution. Also, reinforce that the child did the right thing in coming to you. Try to determine, through careful questioning, whether or not the child inadvertently provoked the bully or tried to prevent the attack in any manner. Teach him how to deal with bullying (see student handout, "Dealing with a Bully: Ideas for Students") and how to prevent further incidents.

4. Let the bully or bullies know that their behavior is unacceptable.
    If more than one bully is involved, address them individually; do not give them the *power of numbers*. Adopt a firm, no-nonsense attitude and begin by expressing your displeasure with, and non-acceptance of, the act. Avoid the temptation to allow the bully to "deny" or justify the behavior. Simply state that the behavior is wrong and you consider it intolerable: inform the student of the consequences. Clearly tell the bully *why* the behavior is unacceptable and exactly *what* behavior you expect instead.

5. Report the incident and your handling of it.
    As soon as you have dealt with both parties, report the incident to both parents and principal and/or counsellor. Include in your report exactly how you handled the situation and what consequences you administered.

6. Create a permanent record.
    Using your original jot notes, as well as facts from your interactions with the students involved, finalize your mini-report and place it somewhere secure. You may need it for future reference.

How to Deal with a Bully: Ideas for Students

You can deal with a bully. It is up to you to take a few important steps, then to report any bullying situation to an adult. You will get results! Here is what you can do.

• Do not fight back.
Fighting back will only make the situation worse. Avoid this at all costs.

• Learn some good words for tough situations.
Make eye contact, then in a tough, angry voice, clearly speak to, not shout at, the bully, then quickly walk away. You might say: *No! Go away! This isn't funny! Get lost! Buzz off!*

• Ignore verbal bullying.
It's hard to do, but if possible, as long as it is just verbal teasing, ignore the bully and quickly walk away. Remember that the bully is looking for a scared reaction from you, and if it doesn't come, he will quickly get bored and stop. Be sure to report the situation right away to an adult.

• Stick together.
Stay close to a crowd, or walk with a group of friends. Bullies will be less likely to confront several people together.

• Learn self-defence.
If you are really concerned, ask your parents if you can enroll in a course in self-defence. Although you will probably not need the actual skills, knowing them will increase your self-confidence. That alone may be enough to turn bullies off.

• Do something unexpected.
Bullies expect you to react with fear. Try something totally unexpected, such as humor, and it just might throw them off. For example, say:
• *Wow! You guys are good. I'm outta here!*
• *If you're trying to scare me—it's working!*
Practise before a mirror first.

• Avoid risky situations.
If at all possible, stay away from places where bullies tend to hang out. Play in a different place, or, if bullies are near, stay near a supervising adult.

• Talk—always.
Never be afraid to tell your teachers or any other adults about bullying—whether you're the target or someone else is. It is everyone's responsibility to report bullying, just as much as it is our responsibility to report vandalism or criminal activity.

How to Discourage Bullies from Inappropriate Behaviors

Remember that bullies are not only modeling behaviors that they have witnessed, but may also be expressing the negative side of their temperaments. That makes re-education necessary. The following strategies may help to change bullying behaviors.

• Use consequences consistently.
Examples of effective, non-violent consequences include loss of privileges and detentions (especially in-school detentions, where bullies are temporarily removed from social interactions). For repeat offenders, removal from the school environment may be necessary.

• Increase supervision of probable bullies.
Once a bully has been identified, or even suspected, be vigilant in supervising that student. Teacher visibility is a great preventative.

• Teach positive alternative behavior.
Teach, in class or as a special, individual session, alternatives to aggressive behavior. Specifically, list behaviors considered inappropriate, such as name-calling, together with alternatives, such as walking away or ignoring. Point out the negative consequences of inappropriate behavior, and liberally praise non-violent behavior. Re-educating students whose behavior has been at fault is sometimes enough to curb bullying.

• Keep communication open.
Let both bullies and their parents know that the lines of communication will be kept open. If further instances of bullying occur, notify parents immediately.

• Have bullies complete a social skills unit.
As part of a consequence of the inappropriate behavior, a bully can be required to complete a mini-unit on social skills. Depending on the grade level, you might ask for a story, written paper, or research project. In some schools, packages are written by individual teachers or by the counsellor and are available in the office. If none are available in your school, consider photocopying pages from any Health unit and having them ready for instant use.

• Use in-class flexible groupings.
Integrating any bully with less aggressive children in groups, where group members must work together towards a common goal, helps promote healthy social skills.

• Utilize one-on-one conferencing.
Let bullies know that aggressive behavior will not be tolerated and that you will be meeting with them regularly (set up a schedule) to discuss their behaviors. Do not accept denial on the part of any bully. Attempt to change the bully's attitude first, then the behavior.

Ways to Take a School-wide Stance Against Bullying

A school that recognizes and embraces bullying as an important issue will reduce the problem more successfully than one that simply deals with individual incidents. There is power in a whole-school approach: students will report bullying more readily, and students inclined to bully will be less likely to act inappropriately.

- Be open to students reporting bullying incidents.
  At all times adult listeners should be compassionate, respectful, non-judgmental, and supportive of student reporters.

- Model positive behavior.
  Teachers should model non-aggressive behaviors, especially when dealing with bullies.

- Make consequences public.
  Everyone, parents included, should be aware of the consequences of bullying. Clear, effective, non-aggressive consequences must be established and implemented consistently.

- Teach and reinforce social skills at every level of development.
  Classes, at every grade, should include lessons on friendship skills, respect, appropriate reporting (as opposed to "tattling"), conflict management, conversational skills, and dealing with bullying.

- Reduce tolerance for bullying.
  By regularly discussing the negative effects of bullying, and equating bullying with such issues as vandalism and criminal offences, tolerance for it will be reduced.

- Utilize class meetings.
  The issue of bullying should be discussed at regular class meetings so that the topic remains relevant and open, and students feel comfortable reporting incidents.

- Have each class create specific rules against bullying and post them.

- Praise pro-social behaviors.
  Whole-school recognition and praise of pro-social behaviors help to create an overall positive environment, where tolerance for bullying is lessened.

- Improve communication.
  Improving communication between home, school, principal, administrators, and students helps to decrease the incidents of bullying, since the potential bullies know they are less likely to get away with inappropriate behaviors.

- Establish a strong teacher presence.
  The better the supervision, not just at recess but before and after school as well, the less the bullying. High adult visibility will deter bullying.

Tips for Students on Making and Keeping Friends

In and out of class you will make friends. Here are some reminders on how to do that—and to keep them too.

• Be yourself.
Perhaps the most important rule for making and keeping friends is to be yourself. No one wants to be friends with someone who is insincere, someone who is "different" with different people, or someone who shows many different "faces."

• Be honest.
Friends need to know they can believe you. This means saying what you mean and meaning what you say. Even "little white lies" can cause you trouble, and you can be sure that any bigger ones will come back to haunt you.

• Be loyal.
Being true to your friends is so important. No one likes a person who quickly flits from one "friend" to another depending on the situation. A good friend needs to be cherished and appreciated.

• Be dependable.
Friends need to be able to count on each other. If you say you will be somewhere or do something, then keep your word.

• Be trustworthy.
It is important that friends can trust each other. Avoid any temptation to gossip or to "two-time" your friend, even if the immediate rewards seem inviting. If trust is lost, it is difficult, if not impossible, to rebuild.

• Be a good listener.
Friendship is two-way. It's great to have a friend who listens to all your problems, but you must listen well in return. This means *really* hearing what is being said, maintaining eye contact, and trying to truly understand and appreciate the concerns of another.

• Share decision making.
You don't always have to be in control, to make all the decisions, or to have the final word. Think of how the other person is feeling or how you would feel in a similar situation.

• Be appreciative.
Tell your friend how much you enjoy, appreciate, and need his or her friendship. There is never a wrong time for positive talk. Nor can there be too much of it. It's OK to tell someone you really care.

• Be forgiving.
Being able to forgive is a loving, mature action. Friendships can follow a rocky road. Sometimes, things are good; sometimes, not so good. People make mistakes so be willing to forgive and forget. By the same token, be prepared to apologize yourself, when necessary.

• Be a giver and a receiver.
In a friendship, there is both giving and receiving. Some people are better at one than the other, and this can put a strain on a relationship. Figure out which you are best at, then work on the other aspect. Consider all aspects of the friendship, including thoughts, feelings, suggestions, constructive criticism, compliments, support, and caring.

4

Teaching Through Hooks, Games, and Fun

Considering all the things that you have to deal with daily as well as the ever-expanding, impossible-to-cover curriculum, you may think it foolish for me to include a chapter on "having fun in the classroom." However, if you think back to your own school years, what do you remember? What times stand out in your mind? When did you learn the most easily? Without a doubt, the answers will somehow include "fun."

When students are having fun, they learn more quickly, waste less time, and remember more. You cannot teach everything from a game format, but the inclusion of some game-type teaching activities can enhance the learning environment within your classroom. Ultimately, they will save you disciplining and reviewing time, which can be better spent working one-on-one with students.

The fun activities, including games and interesting motivational "hooks" for lessons that are featured in this chapter, reinforce curriculum, as well as allow students to practise social skills, such as cooperation, empathy, and sharing. In addition, the activities themselves often include a desirable element of laughter.

You need to have ready access to such invigorating activities, but probably do not have time to create them. This chapter suggests entertaining behaviors, actions, and techniques that can be used within a lesson to reinforce specific content and also between lessons to energize and motivate. Some activities call for a little preparation on the part of the teacher, but most simply require following directions.

The learning will be evident. Students will willingly and enthusiastically take part in cooperative games, such as Theme Think, where generalized concepts are reviewed and practised. They will be learning, without even being aware that they are. And when their attention is captured by simple techniques, such as the use of a music cue or a whispered direction, the lesson will go more smoothly with less need for you to repeat directions or call for attention. Each of these activities reviews, reinforces, or practises an important skill or strategy. When you consider the on-task attention that they promote, they are true time-savers.

Testing, One, Two—May I Have Your Attention, Please?

Every teacher knows there is no point in trying to teach a lesson until all the students (or at least *most* of them) are focusing and paying attention. This doesn't just *happen*. It requires conscious effort on your part. No doubt you are familiar with the flicking-off-the-lights and raised-hand procedures, but these only work until about Grade 2. The following are suggested cues that, when used *consistently*, will help you quickly gain class attention and focus—at all grades. It is not recommended that they all be used, but rather that you select one or two and stick to those. Like any practice, however, novelty is important. If the selected cue appears to be losing its effectiveness, then try a new one. The following list shows how to teach a cue so that it is effective.

How to Teach a Cue

1. Discuss the purpose of an attention cue or signal.

2. Demonstrate the chosen cue.

3. Teach the appropriate reaction to the cue. For example:

   "When you hear/see this signal, return to your desks, sit quietly and listen for what we will do next."

4. Practise the cue several times.

5. Reinforce quick responses to the cue. Tangible rewards, such as candy or tokens, may be necessary during the "training" period.

6. Praise students for making the appropriate response to the cue every time they do so.

   "Thank you for returning to your seats and listening quietly as soon as you saw my signal."

7. Use the cue consistently.

8. Prohibit the students from using or playing with any object used for cueing. Keep the object solely for your use, thereby maintaining its integrity as an official attention-getter.

9. Review periodically the reasons for the cue, as well as your expectations for appropriate behavior(s).

Attention-Getting Cues

Cues can be visual or auditory or both, as long as they are quick and compelling. The following cues have worked for my colleagues and me, from Kindergarten to college level.

Noise Cues

- Whistle for your work.

  Yes, the good old physical education whistle works so much better than shouting. Train students to a simple code. One short blast means "*I need your attention.*" Two blasts means "*Sit down now.*" Three blasts means "*I am getting angry. Pay attention!*" Surprisingly, use of a whistle in a classroom does not disturb neighboring classes. Shouting does!

- Bring the class to order.

  Toy hammers or gavels, found in most dollar stores or toy stores, are an excellent cue. Large and colorful, they usually have a squeak or noise when tapped on the desk or your hand. They are an effective attention-getter, even with adults.

- Attract attention with party sounds.

  A party "blower," readily found in novelty stores, can become a class cue. There are lots available for New Year's Eve. If you choose this type of noisemaker, have extras available as they don't last long.

- Shake, rattle, and call for quiet.

  Any small can, with a few pebbles, pennies, or marbles inside and the top sealed with wide duct tape or packing tape, makes an instant "shaker." (An empty soup can works well.) You can even have one of the students decorate the shaker with paint or paper. Simply give the container a shake when you want attention. So much better than shouting!

- Start the sequence.

  A previously taught set of about three sharp claps, repeated several times if necessary, can be used to gain the class's attention. If desired, students can join in the clap sequence, thereby showing they are ready to listen. Once students have internalized the cue, you can constantly change the sequence. Students must then not only stop what they are doing, but listen carefully so as to mimic the claps.

- Strike a glass.

  This very simple technique is borrowed from the wedding tradition of clinking spoons on glasses to encourage the bride and groom to kiss. Clink a pencil or ruler on a glass (or candy container or pencil holder) to get the class's attention. As before, the initial teaching, practising, and reinforcing of the technique is what makes it work.

Voice Cues

- Whisper, whisper.

  Whisper simple directions to the class. For example: *"Please sit down and listen to what I have to tell you. If you can hear me, put your hands together on your desk."* Students will stop what they are doing and strain to listen. No one, it seems, wants to miss out on a secret. Although this cue doesn't work all the time, it is an excellent novel change from whatever cue has been taught and practised.

- Count down for quiet.

  After thorough teaching of this signal, say loudly, *"You have 3 seconds"* (or whatever). Then the countdown begins—loudly and clearly—3, 2, 1. Start with your voice very loud, gradually getting softer as you count. Students love the challenge of becoming silent before you reach zero.

Silent Cue

- Stop silently.

  Create a STOP sign, a copy of a real one, and attach it to a short handle or stick. Train the class to freeze, return to desks, and attend to you when you stand and raise the sign. This cue works best with younger children and also strengthens their appreciation of a stop sign.

Musical Cues

- Tempt with tunes.

  This cue assumes that the teacher has ready access to a tape deck or CD player. A piece of music, chosen either by the class or the teacher, becomes the signal. As soon as students hear it, they follow the required directions. It is seldom necessary to play more than a few seconds of the tune, although occasionally, it is fun to listen to the entire tune. I find the tape better than the CD; you can have it already cued and push Play whenever you want to. "Baby Elephant Walk," "Pink Panther," and "Peter Gunn," by Mancini, as well as the theme from *Mission Impossible* or almost any selection from *Fantasia*, work well.

- Be a music maestro.

  Any instrument, especially a rhythm band instrument such as a tambourine or hand cymbal, works well. Even a toy xylophone can provide an effective cue. I knew one teacher who effectively used an old recorder. She couldn't play it; she simply gave it a brief blast when she wanted attention.

- Open the music box.

  If you are fortunate enough to have a music box, use it. Children love the sound that music boxes make so they make amazing cues for attention. Keep the box on your desk. It is not a toy for students; it is a teacher cue.

Look at Me: Quick Fixes for Starting Lessons and Boosting Spirit

Here is a variety of snappy motivators for starting lessons.

Auditory Boosters

• Persuasive Words

Ask students to persuade you to give them something like a pencil or chocolate bar. They present their "best" argument in 20 seconds or less. Listen for key words that will lead to the lesson objectives. For example: words such as *poverty* and *no breakfast* for a Social Studies lesson on cultural differences; words such as *equal* and *parts* for a Math lesson on fractions.

• Jokes and Cartoons

Starting a lesson with a joke, whether told or shown on the overhead (newspaper cartoons, for example) and read to the class, can set the stage for a good lesson. *Useable* humor can be a lifesaver, especially with Junior High students.

• Amusing Anecdotes

Students love to hear teacher stories. Share (or create) an anecdote to introduce a lesson. For example, describe how you learned to drive to lead into a Math lesson on sequence or how you got lost to lead into a Language Arts lesson on reading directions.

• Powerful Poetry

A good poem can set the scene for a variety of lessons, from Mathematics to Physical Education. It is even better if you *memorize* the poem and present it. Students will listen in awe. You tie the message of the poem to the lesson. For example, "If" by Rudyard Kipling could lead into a Health lesson on family relationships or growing up, or a Language Arts lesson on the power of poetry.

• Mood-setting Music

Playing a short excerpt of music can instantly set the mood for a variety of types of lessons. For example: the *William Tell Overture* could introduce a Social Studies lesson on wars and fights or a Language Arts lesson on mood and tone.

Visual Boosters

• Bubbles and Sparklers
Children are instantly attracted by bright, colorful visuals such as bubbles and sparklers. These items can be used to provoke interest and questions such as "Why do they reflect all the colors?" or to create a common experience for discussion or descriptive writing projects. Party favors, dollar store gifts, stuffed toys, dolls, and interesting knickknacks all serve the same purpose.

Note: Huge bubbles can be made by combining 1 part glycerin, 1 part Sunlight dish detergent, and 2 parts water. You can make a large circle out of a coat hanger.

• The Big Bag
Rather than just beginning a lesson, pull a carefully chosen item out of a big bag and ask students to guess what the lesson will be about. For example: tape could lead to a Science lesson on properties of adhesion, a Language Arts lesson on singular/plural verb connections, or a Social Studies lesson on how times have changed (settlers didn't have tape).

• Hat Tricks
Even just donning a hat will usually get an immediate response from a class. The creative use of a hat can be an instant motivator. For example, wearing a sunhat could lead into a Health lesson on body awareness or a Social Studies lesson on caste systems. Start a collection and keep your hats in a cupboard for instant use.

Thought Boosters

• Imaginative Experiences
Ask students to sit comfortably and close their eyes. Tell them to breathe deeply and slowly, then take them through a series of steps in which they imagine they are in a location that leads to the lesson. For example: walking through a pioneer town leads into a Social Studies lesson on early settlers; sitting beside a clear pond, where water suddenly turns brown, leads into a Science lesson on pollution; walking through a dark, scary forest leads into a Language Arts lesson on setting.

• Thought Targets
Children are quickly motivated by these simple activities. Since you know the objective and content of the lesson, give the topic and the directions. Ask students working alone or in partners to think of as many related items as they can. For example, if you're planning a lesson on verbs, say, "Think of all words that begin with 'v.'" First student or pair to guess *verb* wins.

Thought targets usually centre on the following: words that start with the letter, words that rhyme with a certain word, all things similar in some way (color, shape, use, size), or words related to a theme (change, loss, gain).

Let's Play: A Menu of Ten Teaching Games

Children learn through games. Even the word "game" seems to pique interest and focus attention. The games featured here are innovative ways for teaching communication skills, as well as social skills such as cooperation, empathy, and sharing. They can be used within a lesson to reinforce content and also between lessons to energize and motivate. All can easily be followed up with a writing activity.

- Theme Think
  A take-off of a popular TV quiz show, this partner activity involves thinking about concepts, as well as concentrating on verbal communication skills. (See page 58.)

- Play-It-Again Paper Plate Band
  Children of all ages love this engaging activity which quickly gets rid of excess energy while reinforcing careful looking and rhythm skills. (See page 58.)

- Once-Again Stories
  This game is sure to bring laughter. It involves listening and speaking skills, as well as memory and often creativity. It encourages public speaking. (See page 59.)

- That's the Rule
  This game demands careful attention to details as well as good questioning strategies. The level of difficulty can be altered for different ages. (See page 60.)

- Double Interviews
  Some children like to perform; some like to be in the audience. This activity, which promotes careful listening, allows for both. (See page 60.)

- Muddling Anyone?
  It involves careful thinking before speaking as well as good questioning techniques and even better answers. It can also be used to teach the concept of verbs. (See page 61.)

- Deskward Bound
  Children periodically need to get up and move around. This activity capitalizes on this in a way that can be both stimulating and entertaining. (See page 61.)

- Repeated Mime
  This activity links the concept of storytelling through mime with the necessity for watching carefully. The results can be hilarious. (See page 62.)

- Folded Stories
  This whole-class activity involves thinking, writing, and reading. (See page 62.)

- How Is It Done?
  This game reinforces an understanding of adverbs. (See page 63.)

Theme Think

Type of Game: Partner
Preparation: On overheads or chalkboard, write lists of words related to a specific theme.
How to Play

1. The partner who has to guess the words covers eyes or turns back to board or overhead.
2. The other person provides word clues without using hand movements or saying any part of the desired word. For example, looking at "cowboy," the partner might say, "He rides a horse."
3. The first set of partners to meet the challenge wins.

Extension: Challenges are fun. Partners can challenge other partners and let the class "bet" who they think will win.

Examples of Words on a Theme

SPORTS	WEATHER
Hockey soccer baseball basketball jersey goal stick hoop cleats club puck mitt uniform referee umpire fans	Snow fog blizzard sun hot cold rain tornado hurricane thunder ice wind gale lightning clouds

Examples of Themes

school	girls' names	boys' names
at home	science terms	math functions
at the mall	hobbies	healthy foods
friends	fast foods	animals

Play It Again Paper Plate Band

Type of Game: Whole class
Preparation: Obtain enough paper plates to provide two per student plus a lively tape (*William Tell Overture* is great).
How to Play

1. Pass out plates, play music, and have the class keep a rhythm. Children love doing this, it uses up lots of energy, and it brings smiles and laughter.
2. Different students can take turns "leading" the style of keeping the rhythm.

Examples of Possible Ways to Keep the Rhythm
• Use plates as cymbals.
• Tap plates on legs, head, or shoulders.
• Put plates together to form duck bills, mouse ears, antlers, whatever, and move in rhythm.
• Clap plates together to one side, then the other; then up, then down.
• Clap or "swish" plates together quickly or slowly or melodramatically.

Once-Again Stories

Type of Game: Whole class, with three or four students asked to step outside of class for a moment

Preparation: See Note below.

How to Play

1. With the four students out of the room, the teacher (or student) tells a short story, real or imagined, to the class.
2. One student enters and a volunteer retells the story to him.
3. The second student enters, and student one retells the story to him and so on. The final telling of the story is always different from the first.
4. The original storyteller retells the true story so that everyone can see the differences.

Note: It may be a good idea to have an original story written as a first step in this activity. Invite each student to write 50–100 words. Collect all stories and save unused ones for future use. Encourage students to include lots of description, as this is what makes the retelling more fun.

Example of a Short Story for the Telling

One dark night Benny was walking through the terrible forest when he met a strange little character, not more than one metre tall, and the character's pet squirrel. The character was called Lenny, and his squirrel was Kenny. He begged Benny to help him find his way home. Lenny's home was in an old tree stump, but because of the dark he couldn't find it. Together they walked for hours, through vines, bushes, and mud, and over rocks and huge tree roots, but they couldn't find Lenny and Kenny's tree. Eventually, Benny decided to take the little man and his squirrel home with him; however they all realized they were lost. All night long they trudged through the dark and frightening forest. Finally they came to an opening in the trees where a lovely little cottage sat proudly. It was all lit up under a single moonbeam and was uninhabited. Deciding to remain there, Benny, the tall one, Lenny, the small one, and Kenny, the even smaller one, became known as the forest's mystery men.

That's the Rule

Type of Game: Whole class
Preparation: None
How to Play

1. One student leaves the room.
2. The class chooses a "rule" (see below for suggestions).
3. The student returns to the room and asks questions about the rule to which class members reply either "yes" or "no." (Students answer according to the selected rule.)
4. After three wrong guesses, the guesser is out. He can either choose someone to help him guess the next rule, or can "give away" the guesser position to another. (Everyone wants to be the guesser.)

Examples of Rules
• Every other person says "no," no matter what the question is.
• Girls all say "no."
• People wearing red say "no."
• Always preface an answer by coughing.
• Always preface an answer by bending forward slightly.
• All those with glasses say "yes."
• Always answer the opposite of the truth.
• Every third person says "no."
• Respondents touch their faces as they answer.
• Respondents look away from the guesser while answering

Note: The best way to guess the rule is to ask several people the same question, for example, "Are you a boy?" Students will then answer according to the rule, and it will eventually become obvious what that rule is.

Double Interviews

Type of Game: Groups of three
Preparation: None
How to Play

1. Supply a reason for an interview (see below).
2. The person in the middle is the interviewer who must talk to both people at the same time and not lose the sequence of either interview.
3. People being interviewed act as if there is no "third" person. They constantly try to throw the interviewer off target with responses or questions that conflict with what the other interviewee is saying.

Possible Interview Reasons

For a job at a department store
For a maid service
For a position as nanny
For a dog walker

For a butler
For a hula dancer
For a weightlifter
For a rock band guitar player

Muddling Anyone?

Type of Game: Whole class
Preparation: None
How to Play
1. One person, the seeker, leaves.
2. The class decides on an action word, that is, a verb (see below for suggestions).
3. The seeker returns and asks questions in an attempt to discover the selected verb (see below for sample questions).
4. Students must respond without giving away the exact verb; instead, they use the word *muddle.* They give true answers, as these are the clues for the seeker. Example: Seeker asks, "Where do you muddle?" The student who has been asked replies, "I muddle at home every day." The selected word was *study.*
5. Once the seeker has the word, he chooses the next seeker.

Possible Actions

skate	bathe	smile
eat	swim	breathe
sing	dance	read

Possible Questions
- When do you muddle?
- Do you like muddling?
- Do you muddle alone?
- Where do you muddle?
- How often do you muddle?
- Do you use your hands to muddle?

Note: Once students understand this game, they quickly generate their own questions. Answers can be hilarious.

Deskward Bound

Type of Game: Whole class, requiring in-class movement
Preparation: None
How to Play
1. Ask all students to move as far away from their own desks as possible.
2. Provide students with directions for returning to their own desks. There is no challenge here, but lots of fun and creative "getting rid of excess energy."

Ways to Move
- Crawl back.
- Return using three body parts on the floor.
- Return with eyes closed.
- Hop or dance.
- Take as few steps as possible.
- Take the most direct route, the least direct route.
- Slide forwards or sidewards.
- Move like a crab.
- Do the moon walk.
- Walk as if on the moon (less gravity).
- Move as if you have a broken leg.

Repeated Mime

Type of Game: Whole class, with three students asked to step outside for a moment
Preparation: None
How to Play
   1. The class decides on an action, and an actor is chosen (see below for ideas).
   2. One student returns, watches mime, then repeats what she saw to the next person and so on. Hilarious!

Possible Actions

changing a tire
making cookies, bread, or pie
playing a sport
visiting the dentist
caught in a thunderstorm
washing a car
hanging wallpaper

changing a dirty diaper
doing a science experiment
driving a car
taking a shower
walking a dog (or several dogs)
bathing a dog

Note: This game is the same as "Once-Again Stories," except that it is done in mime.

Folded Stories

Type of Game: Groups of at least six (if the class is in rows, use one row as a group)
Preparation: None
How to Play
   1. Group members sit in a line or row.
   2. Each group has a piece of paper folded into as many sections as there are group members.
   3. As the teacher, you provide the first line or general theme (see below).
   4. The first person writes a sentence about the topic and hands the folded paper to the second.
   5. The second person cannot see what has been written, but must write what he/she thinks will come next, and so on.
   6. Writings are shared with the entire class.

Examples of Themes

Class members going to the mall
A trip to the movies
A party

Three students going camping
A first date between two class members
The scariest night for two class members

How Is It Done?

Similar to "Muddling Anyone?" this game involves an understanding of adverbs. With younger children adverbs can be explained as "describing words that tell how an activity is performed." The game is a good tool for reinforcing this concept.

Type of Game: Whole class, with one person, the guesser, stepping out
Preparation: Make sure that the class has a basic understanding of what adverbs are.
How to Play
1. The class decides on an adverb, for example, slowly. Other suggestions include anxiously, confidently, clumsily, carefully, happily, sadly, tiredly, and energetically.
2. The guesser returns and asks specific students to carry out simple activities according to the chosen adverb. For example: "Walk to the door." The student who has been asked to walk goes *slowly.*
3. The guesser is allowed no more than three questions before he must make a guess.
4. If he guesses incorrectly, he chooses a helper to assist with the next guess, *or* the teacher selects a different guesser. If the guesser is correct, he selects the next guesser.

5

Tapping into Creativity: Quick Activities, Assemblies, and Art

Creativity makes the humdrum appealing. In teaching, it makes the good teacher better. Even the simplest lesson can be delivered creatively. Old material can be revisited creatively and new material presented creatively.

So much of the required curriculum can be, well, boring. So, when seeking ways for students to reinforce or practise skills, you will want to turn to more imaginative measures. Any activity where children are involved is a learning pursuit. However, you do need activities that not only support your teaching, but that don't consume too much time or pose difficulties in overseeing. Whatever tasks you come up with must, therefore, be designed so that students can complete them, or at least work on them, largely on their own. That will leave you with precious moments to meet individual children's needs.

This chapter offers ideas for highly motivating student activities that will work well all year, with a minimum of preparation or supervision on your part. Students will be actively engaged; they will be reviewing attitudes, skills, and knowledge without even being aware that they are doing so. In addition, they will be using their own creativity to complete the suggested projects, some of which will become prized student "take-homes."

The chapter also considers school assemblies and suggests ways to "spice them up." These important, but often less than exciting gatherings will be more attention-grabbing if, for example, talents are showcased or school spirit activities are featured. Assemblies that are given some creative thought and energy might be more educational and will certainly be more entertaining.

A similar area of concern for many teachers is the school concert. I often hear teachers bemoaning an upcoming concert. They are at a loss for ideas and feel unskilled in the areas of music and drama. But concerts are fun and do not need to generate anxiety. Nor do they need to be gala productions. Children are natural performers; point them in the right direction and they will do the rest. This chapter therefore includes a list of possible concert activities for Kindergarten to Grade 9 that even the least musical teacher can easily direct. Take the headache out of your next school concert. Read on!

The final area of creativity addressed in this chapter is art. How often have you found yourself rushing around trying to put together an art lesson at the last minute? Where are those easy art lessons when you need them? This chapter offers ten of them; each lesson is a simple, paper-and-pencil activity that requires no preparation and no clean-up. In addition, the lessons all promote manual dexterity, creativity, and imagination, and fit nicely into existing art curriculums.

A Menu of Fun Learning Activities

These classroom-tested activities can be used at any time during the school year, but have proved especially successful for the last two weeks of school.

- Memories in the Making
  Children love to take something of importance home at the end of the year. Have them develop collections of "memories," including drawings, good assignments, photocopies of candid photos, journal entries, and written reviews of field trips. (See page 67.)

- Blow Your Mind Brainstorming
  Since children are naturally creative, they will enjoy not only offering ideas at random, but creatively organizing them as well. (See page 68.)

- Testimony to Our Time
  Students love the feeling of being wiser than those to follow them. Ask each of them to create a visual of some sort—a legacy—for next year's class. (See page 69.)

- Time in a Box
  The whole concept of passing time and looking into the future is intriguing to children. Capitalize on this by creating a class time capsule that will contain carefully selected mementoes of the year. (See page 69.)

- Poster Perfect
  All children enjoy creating large, colorful posters, especially with a partner or in small groups. (See page 71.)

- A Day for Showing Off
  Showing off comes naturally to children. Capitalize on this and have a day where each student is encouraged to show off a skill, talent, article, or idea. (See page 72.)

- Signed, Sealed, and Delivered
  Children will enjoy writing to someone who can provide answers to real or imagined problems. Have a "Dear Abby" day. (See page 73.)

- A Mural for the Showing
  Children love to be noticed. As a class, create a huge mural that can be displayed where all will see and appreciate it. (See page 74.)

- Rhythm Band
  Children love to make noise, and, yes, you can actually create a home-made rhythm band through this fun activity. (See page 75.)

- Scavenger Hunt
  Don't overlook this wonderful, whole-class activity. (See page 75.)

Memories in the Making

Object: To have each student prepare a book of memories

Teacher Involvement: Some supervision of Memory book preparation

Student Accountability: The possession of the finished product motivates students and promotes accountability.

Duration: Several hours spread over days or weeks

Curriculum Connection: Language Arts, Art, as well as review of all core subjects

Steps

1. Collect duotangs or coiled books or have an aide coil a book for each child.
2. Provide each child with a piece of colored construction paper for the cover.
3. Invite students to decorate the construction paper, then glue the finished covers to the front of their books.
4. Keep these books in a special container, readily accessible to all.
5. Introduce the concept of a Memory book.
6. As a class, brainstorm what could go into one.
7. Tell students to give each page a different name according to subjects and various special activities. For example, there might be pages for Science, Mathematics, a field trip to the zoo, a Christmas time party, or a Halloween parade.
8. Ask students to pass their books around. Every student writes or illustrates something that comes to mind related to the page. For example, student A might draw the same cartoon on everybody's Science page, while student B might write a joke about what happened in a Science class.
9. It will take some time for the books to circulate completely. When students are finished routine work, they can choose to work on a Memory book, or you can incorporate Memory book periods into the week.
10. If you have taken any candid photos during the year, photocopy them and give them to the students; they can glue these onto pages in their Memory books.
11. Individuals can add to their own books by putting in well done assignments, pictures, and so on.
12. Reserve the last couple of pages are for the ever-popular "signatures."

Blow Your Mind Brainstorming

Object: To thoroughly review past learning and class experiences
Teacher Involvement: No preparation, just in-class supervision
Student Accountability: Increases when task is turned into a "game"
Duration: About an hour, depending on how far the game is taken
Curriculum Connection: All subjects in review; Language Arts for writing

This whole-class, in-class activity works well for any day in the last week. Sometimes it is good to do this before work on the Memory book. Simply ask students to brainstorm responses to an initiating question such as, "Let's think of all the things we learned in Social Studies this year." Once students get going, the brainstorming can last for a long time—they may recall some of the tiniest details. This activity also serves as a good memory refresher about just how much they have learned during the year. You might make the question open-ended, for example, "What do you remember most about this year?" and responses can include all the funny, sad, happy, unusual, or exciting things that happened whether or not they had anything do with actual curriculum.

Steps
1. Divide the class into groups of about five students.
2. Each group is given about four pieces of chart paper.
3. Each piece is labeled according to subjects, field trips, activities, or specific topics such as types of insects or behaviors of wild geese.
4. On a start cue, groups fills each sheet with as many facts as they can recall about each topic.
5. At the end of a set time, tally the number of responses to find a winner (if you want it to be in game format). Otherwise, use the charts for discussion. There can be a separate winner for each category, for example, Science, as well as an overall winner.
6. Have students circle the most important points on their charts.
7. Ask a representative from each group to present the important points.
8. Prepare and display a final whole-class chart.

Testimony to Our Time

Object: To pass on useful information to the next class

Teacher Involvement: Initial instruction, no preparation

Student Accountability: Intrinsic for many who will want to leave a legacy; heighten the accountability of others by offering rewards, such as candy, for completed legacies.

Duration: Varies according to age; usually at least an hour

Curriculum Connection: Language Arts, Art

Steps

1. Begin by teaching the meaning of the word legacy. (A legacy is something handed down from one who has gone before.)
2. Discuss why it would be a good idea to leave a legacy for the upcoming students. (What do you know now that you didn't at the beginning of the year? What tips can you give next year's students?)
3. Provide students with paper, glue, coloring mediums, and old magazines.
4. Ask students to write poems or short captions that will tell incoming students something about this class.
5. Students should decorate pages in any way they see fit.
6. Arrange for an aide or volunteer to laminate completed pages. Doing so ensures page preservation, and students really love to see their work treated this way.
7. Post legacies, and you will have a ready display for the following year.

Time in a Box

Object: To determine objects that represent students' learning and experiences that year

Teacher Involvement: Collection of box and art type materials; supervision only; students will work on their own.

Student Accountability: Intrinsic because they love the idea. If further accountability is required, provide a little reward for completion of each part.

Duration: Can take several hours, depending on capsule contents

Curriculum Connection: All subjects in review, Language Arts, Art

Steps

1. Introduce the concept of a time capsule for students who will be in this class sometime in the future. "What should we leave that will say something about us and what we did this year?"
2. Show the empty box that will become the time capsule. Keep it fairly small; a shoebox works well.
3. Brainstorm for a possible list of items to be included.
4. Have older students complete the time capsule worksheet (next page).
5. Select candidates to find each item to be put in the capsule. Everyone must have something to put in.
6. Allow students to work on their own or in small groups.
7. Delegate one group to decorate the actual box.
8. Call upon the entire class to arrange completed items in the box.
9. Have the class select one student who will prepare a written list of objects/items.
10. Ask selected delegates to present the closed time capsule to the principal.

Time Capsule: Student Worksheet

What do you think should be put in the time capsule? Check your favorites. Put an * beside the one item on which you would most like to work.

❑   Class pictures or cartoons of members _____

❑   Class true story (what we really did this year—can include any funny happenings)

_____

❑   Class fiction story (create us a story about our class) _____

❑   Poems about Grade ___ _____

❑   Pictures about our class _____

❑   Collages on what we did this year _____

❑   A map of what our class looks like _____

❑   Interviews with class members _____

Possible questions

What did you like best about this school year?

What was your best/worst memory?

What was your best/worst subject?

What did you like/dislike about the class setup?

❑   Technology report (how used …?) _____

❑   Favorite recess or after-class activities _____

❑   Description of class banner or flag _____

❑   Inclusion of class rules and/or Bills of Rights _____

❑   Any special items, such as pens, pencils, and mascots _____

❑   Photocopy of a report card (artificially filled in) _____

❑   Other ideas? _____

_____

Poster Perfect

Object: To produce effective posters that review, in advertising format, something that happened during the year

Teacher Involvement: Provision of materials and supervision only

Student Accountability: Largely intrinsic, but motivators can be offered in the form of candy or tokens of appreciation, such as stickers, erasers, or pencils

Duration: Up to two hours, depending on age and interest of students

Curriculum Connection: Concept review, Art, Language Arts, problem solving

Steps
1. Introduce the concept of a poster that advertises something (a subject, a specific concept, a special event, your class as a whole) by highlighting key or most important ideas or points.
2. Discuss the effects of different mediums. For example, felt markers create a bolder, more vibrant poster which might show the excitement of a physical education class, whereas pencil crayons can create a softer, more subtle effect, which might suggest the more thoughtful side of Language Arts. A combination of mediums can also be effective, for example, to differentiate between a background illustration and foreground text.
3. Discuss the importance of keeping a poster simple; it should display only one main idea.
4. Select (or have a pre-selected) topic. For example, the posters could represent a subject area or an event, but not both.
5. Brainstorm for possible ideas about the chosen topic. How many ideas that could be shown on the poster can the students remember about the topic?
6. Chart the ideas (on board or chart paper).
7. Ask each student, pair of students, or small group to review the chart and write down exactly what idea(s) they will present.
8. Direct the poster-making teams to select mediums to use. Provide them with large pieces of paper or card. (Bristol board works well; it is firm and easy to color.)
9. Allow students to create posters, using mediums of their choice.
10. Call upon students to present completed posters. Explaining their posters to the class is an important part of the whole communication process.
11. Display posters, and plan to use them next year as well.

A Day for Showing Off

Object: To promote communication skills and self-esteem

Teacher Involvement: Supervision; no preparation

Student Accountability: Intrinsic, as most love to show off. With this activity, however, it may be wise to allow the few who do not wish to participate to be "judges."

Duration: Can last for several hours depending on class

Curriculum Connection: Communication and listening skills

Steps

1. Explain that each student will be given time to show off in front of the class something that they have learned this year. It may be something from school or outside of it (a dance move, a guitar solo, a math problem, how to serve a volleyball).
2. Discuss whether or not the class wishes to invite another class to witness their "show-offs."
3. Brainstorm for possible skills, talents, or learnings to show off.
4. Give students a few days to "prepare," either at school or at home.
5. Do a pre-check to be sure that all students have something. Be prepared to make suggestions to those who don't seem to have anything. Perhaps they have "pet rock," a good assignment, or a special moment with a grandparent to share.
6. Have a practice run, especially if you are going to invite another class.
7. If you wish, invite another class to watch your show-offs, and offer to watch theirs.
8. If some students don't want to participate, respect their privacy or "shyness." Allow them to be judges, and select a winner for the best show-off. Judges can act as a sort of jury, just so that they are involved. They might complete a chart that doesn't actually rank the show-offs, but keeps them, the judges, focused.
9. An alternative way to use the Judges' Scoring Key is to provide all students with enough copies to "score" each show-off. This requirement bumps up audience accountability.

Judges' Scoring Key Worksheet

a. Name _____

b. Description of show-off activity _____

_____

_____

_____

c. How long it took _____

d. How interesting? _____

e. Where learned (at home or at school?) _____

Signed, Sealed, and Delivered

Object: To provide next year's classes with thoughtful advice

Teacher Involvement: Supervision, no preparation

Student Accountability: Intrinsic, but rewards can be offered for completion of at least one letter

Duration: About an hour

Curriculum Connection: Language Arts, Health, problem solving

Steps

1. Tell students about the famous newspaper column "Dear Abby." Perhaps share a section of such an advice column with them.
2. Have students work in pairs.
3. Ask them to write about serious concerns they had when they first entered this grade, class, or school; then, invite them to raise questions they might have now—the latter can be "foolish."
4. Tell partners not to put their names on their questions. Instead, each pair is given a number with which to identify their paper.
5. Papers are collected and distributed randomly.
6. Partners now write an answer, suggestion, or solution to one of the problems in the form of a "Dear Abby" letter.

   Example: Dear Abby, Ever since I came to this class I've been scared of the bigger kids. What should I do about it?

   Signed, "Worried"

   Dear Worried,
   Don't be afraid of them. Just be yourself and they will be nice to you. However, if anyone in particular bothers you, tell the teacher. Be careful not to get into a fight.

7. Papers are then passed on to another pair and so on until all the questions have been responded to.
8. Papers are returned to original owners.
9. Share the letters aloud. Select any questions and responses that should be read to next year's class at the beginning of the year.

A Mural for the Showing

Object: To cooperatively produce a mural on learning experiences
Teacher Involvement: More involvement required here, but the results are well worth it
Student Accountability: Students are highly motivated to do this.
Duration: Can take a whole day if you want it to
Curriculum Connection: Art, cooperation, communication skills, problem solving
Steps

1. Preparation: Tape several large sheets of paper together to create a piece of paper at least two metres by one metre. Leave whole *or* after taping the paper together, cut it up into large jigsaw pieces, numbering each piece as you cut it up *or* simply give each student a single 8" by 11" sheet of paper.
2. Discuss all the things that you have done during the year so far, including curriculum, field trips, and other special activities.
3. Pick a specific topic, for example, Social Studies.
4. Either have students all write, draw, paint, or do whatever they want to anywhere on the whole, uncut mural paper

   or

   select specific students to draw, color, or print specific parts of the general theme (A draws a pioneer; B records some important dates.)

   or

   give pairs or small groups a piece of the jigsaw puzzle. They decorate it in any way they want (encourage full coloring of the piece), keeping to the topic or theme. Pieces are finally taped back together forming a wonderful tapestry.
   Note: This is my favorite. Students love to see the finished product.

   or

   tape all the individual pages together into a crazy quilt.
5. Display the mural and once again you have a wonderful exhibit for the following year.

Rhythm Band

Object: To make rhythm with original instruments

Teacher Involvement: Conducting the "orchestra" and locating the music

Student Accountability: Enjoyment of the finished product is sufficient.

Duration: Once instruments have been collected, only a few minutes at a time are necessary to get the full benefit from this activity.

Curriculum Connection: Music, cooperation, listening skills

Steps
1. Discuss rhythm and rhythm bands.
2. Listen to selected music. (Try to use classical music; you will be increasing their musical repertoire by doing so.)
3. Brainstorm for possible "instruments," for example, two sticks or jingle bells. It's good to have a couple of real rhythm band instruments available, but it's not necessary.
4. Challenge students to find their own instruments during the next few days. Give them a deadline. It may be necessary to reward them tangibly as they bring their instruments to school.
5. Practise the rhythm in the song first by clapping or tapping desks.
6. Create your rhythm band from the found objects, and, if possible, share a rhythm session with another audience, such as the office staff or a peer class.

Scavenger Hunt

Object: To promote cooperative group work

Teacher Involvement: Creation of the hunt (possible list next page)

Student Accountability: Intrinsic, but there should be a prize for first group finished

Duration: Varies

Curriculum Connection: Cooperation, problem solving, communication skills (Inventive children will "make" many of the items, thus expanding the range of skills needed.)

Note: Be sure to get office permission before allowing your students to search for the items on their lists.

Steps
1. Create enough scavenger hunt pages for the class.
2. Have students form into groups of about five.
3. Discuss hunt rules (time, where they can/cannot go, no stealing from other groups, remaining quiet during the search, not bothering other teachers or classes, cooperation).
4. Give groups five minutes to choose names for themselves.
5. Provide each group with an empty bag.
6. Let the groups begin their hunts.

Scavenger Hunt: Student Worksheet

- ❏ A pencil no more than 5 cm long
- ❏ A button
- ❏ An old business letter from the secretary
- ❏ A cupcake
- ❏ A shoe bigger than size 10
- ❏ A feather mop
- ❏ A pail
- ❏ A 100% paper or test
- ❏ A poem about a dog
- ❏ A metre stick
- ❏ A plastic glass
- ❏ A Christmas ornament
- ❏ An old Valentine card
- ❏ A picture of a dog

Weather permitting

- ❏ A _____ leaf
- ❏ A smooth stone
- ❏ A bud
- ❏ A stick exactly 10 cm long
- ❏ Something alive from nature, but not an insect or animal
- ❏ Something dead from nature, but not an insect or animal
- ❏ A seed
- ❏ A feather
- ❏ A flower

Assemblies with Audience Appeal

Assemblies, those wonderful/horrible whole-school meetings in the huge gymnasium, with its appalling acoustics, can be a nightmare. True, they are necessary; they are useful tools for sharing, teaching appropriate audience behavior, creating school cohesiveness and spirit, and, of course, for passing on important information. However, too often each tends to be a drawn-out, boring exercise for the students and a management challenge for the teachers. It doesn't have to be this way. The following are suggestions not only for enlivening the content of the assembly, but also for getting to and from it.

Setting Parameters

• March to the beat.
Using a piece of brisk marching music over the intercom, *march* the classes to the gym, to a pre-assigned seating place. You know the chaos of getting several hundred students into one location. Make the *march* a contest. Which class can arrive the most quickly and be standing in place like soldiers? When the music stops, students sit down.

• Sing first.
Singing sets the stage! Teach, and use faithfully, a school song. There is amazing strength in this action. Make it the customary opening for every assembly. If you do not have someone creative who can write a song especially for your school, rewrite the words to any familiar melody and go from there. Students love it and it creates a sense of school pride.

• Stick to a time limit.
Students (and teachers) need to know just how long an assembly is going to be. Choose an appropriate length of time, and stick to it. Unfinished business? Move it to a future gathering, or find another way in which to share it.

• Appoint student masters of ceremonies.
Use student power. Pre-select two student MCs (different ones for each assembly). Decide on selection criteria, but be sure the students can practise beforehand and can "handle the crowd." Students are much more likely to give full attention to peers than to adults.

• Mix the good and the bad.
Students will turn off if the entire content of an assembly is either negative or in lecture format. Mix reinforcements with warnings—good with bad. Never talk for more than a few minutes on any one topic, especially something negative like misdemeanors.

• Invite parents, neighbors, shopkeepers, and seniors.
Invite all parents to attend all assemblies, but also invite particular parents to the assemblies in which their children are taking part. Inviting storekeepers and neighbors to the school improves community involvement and school-community relationships. Seniors often love to attend, too, and they make a welcome addition to assemblies.

Providing a Showcase

• Showcase a class.

Students like to be a part of a showcased group. At each assembly, a different class might share a "room chant" they have created and practised. If desired, this short and simple choral speech can be accompanied by actions. An example might be

> *Class 5A! Class 5A!*
> *If you want to learn, just come our way.*
> *We keep smiling every day.*
> *We're the best, we just must say!*

• Showcase individual talents.

At each assembly, allow one (or two) students to perform, or to present a specific talent or skill. One teacher should be in charge of auditions, and all "acts" should be previewed. You'll find that many students will want to star at an assembly, and the acts enliven the meeting.

• Recognize pro-social behavior.

At every assembly, ensure that one or two students are acknowledged for specific demonstrations of excellent social behavior. Have a peer, previously selected and coached by staff, do the acknowledgment.

• Consider a surprise guest speaker.

Inviting interesting guest speakers to assemblies is an excellent ploy. There are many persons in the neighborhood, from seniors to police constables to veterinarians to tradespeople, who may be willing to take a few minutes to talk to students. Listening to them will give students a good introduction to a variety of occupations. Just remember to limit any speaker's time.

• Showcase a group or team.

Students love to see who's doing what in their school. Introduce the members of a team or club, but don't stop there. Have each team member "do" something related to the team. For example, the members of the soccer team could mime kicking, heading, goaltending, or blocking. Members of the drama club could assume an instant tableau. Members of the cheer team could do a quick cheer. Caution: Feature only one group per assembly.

• Use staff talent.

Teachers are wonderfully creative actors! Use your own talents to "perform." Sing, dance, tell jokes, or act totally out-of-character. Students will love it and you will reinforce positive teacher-student rapport. If it is *expected* that everyone on staff will be responsible for a two-minute act at one assembly per year, teachers will rise beautifully to the occasion!

Creative Concert Ideas

Every teacher knows the horror of having to come up with an easy-to-handle act for the inevitable school concert. Sure, the drama and music teachers have an edge, but it's not fair to leave all the planning and preparation up to them. Besides, it's one of the highs of teaching to watch your class perform something you have created and directed. Don't miss this opportunity! It doesn't have to be a three-act play or even a perfectly choreographed dance. Children are natural actors. Give them a little guidance and watch them go. The following are ideas that require a minimum of talent, preparation, or practice for at least *interesting* results.

Mainly Movement Ideas

• Shake, beat, and clink.
The age-old rhythm band seems to have lost favor, but it is still a fantastic way for children of all ages to express themselves to music. If you do not have rhythm band equipment, make it. With older students this is half the fun. What can they find that will "make a noise"? Sticks, shakers, lids, bells, metal rods, glasses … Invite them to locate an instrument, choose a song, and away you go!

• Form a marching band.
Young children are great at marching. Have them act like stiff, well-trained soldiers and march in formation across the stage. Add hats made in class, a banner displaying the names of the class members, and a lively marching tune. If you can, provide the leading student with a set of cymbals; the clashing will add interest.

• Create animal images.
Children from Kindergarten to Grade 3 will enjoy acting like animals of their choice. Paint their faces with black noses, whiskers, and so on; add any available costume pieces, perhaps from Halloween; and let them move to music as the animals they are depicting. Music from any of the animated Disney films works well.

• Create eye candy.
Have students draw and color pictures related to a piece of music. Make colored overheads of their art and show these while the music plays. You could also have students sing or create a narration as an accompaniment.

• Move as one.
Synchronized movement is a delight to watch, even when it doesn't work! Choose a simple piece of music and teach the entire group a series of easy movements to accompany it. No ideas? Ask the students to create the movements, or watch a music video or aerobics show on TV.

• Create a shadow play.

Have students create movements, puppet plays, dramatic actions, and so on behind a sheet held up by two class members. When a light such as the one from an overhead projector is shone on the sheet, interesting shadows are created. Invite the students to find a musical selection to accompany their shadow show.

Movement and Speech Ideas

• Speak as one.

Children like to hear their own voices. Capitalize on this by having them memorize a favorite poem and simply present as choral speech. Create interest by breaking the poem into parts and adding actions or simple props. Audiences will love it.

• Rap about it.

Take a simple nursery rhyme or familiar song—and have the class change it completely. Some students can present it in rap, some in opera form, some in mime, and some in country.

• Mime in time.

While a part of the class reads (or presents as memorized verse or text) a short selection, specific students mime the actions. Simple costumes or even just signs pinned on the "actors" add color and interest.

• Let students mimic teachers.

Students love to make fun of their teachers. Older students are great at miming teachers' familiar actions and behaviors. Capitalize on this by creating a simple classroom skit where various students are different teachers, while the others are class members. Be sure to ask permission of the teachers being mimicked beforehand. Usually these are the best-loved teachers, who will readily laugh at themselves.

• Share interesting information.

Challenge older students to find out interesting facts about their school or community, for example, who the first principal was, what famous person attended the school, or how the school population has changed. In pairs or small groups, students simply present these facts in a question-and-answer format. They might also use costume pieces, such as an unusual reporter's hat.

• Play with a parody.

Children of all ages love to make fun of something. Take a simple, familiar poem, nursery rhyme, story, or TV show and together develop a parody of it. I once saw a Grade 3 class present a hilarious parody of the TV show *Friends*. They called it "Enemies" and involved students as directors, camerapeople, make-up artists, and producers. Although it had been scripted, it ended up rather spontaneous.

- Fake a fashion show.

   Challenge students to create the most unusual outfits imaginable (a sheet becomes a toga; a tablecloth—"The perfect veil for today's bride-on-the-go"). Select a few students to narrate, and enjoy a hilarious, no-practice-necessary fashion show.

- Conduct a mock muscleman/beauty contest.

   Here's where role reversals are fun. All the girls take part in a funny "body-builder" display, while the boys, appropriately dressed, are the beauty contestants. A few of the students become the judges, and funny prizes, such as a decorated paper plate, are awarded. The entire contest can be done in less than five minutes, and children love it!

- Rewrite lyrics and sing.

   As a class, write new lyrics to a familiar tune, and present as a choir. Be sure to act serious, carrying books, candles, or whatever. *Take Me Out of the Bathtub and Other Silly Dilly Songs* by Alan Katz is a good resource.

- Present readers' theatre.

   Students from Grade 4 to Grade 9 are especially good at readers' theatre. Select a simple, short story that can be broken into parts, or locate a good readers' theatre book for ideas. Students can practise on their own, add appropriate costume bits, sound effects, and lighting, and present.

- Perform with puppets.

   Help students to create puppets, such as simple paper bag or sock puppets. Arrange the class in a semicircle on the stage with their puppets. Individual puppets can say a short line to the audience in character, or the entire group can perform a choral speech. Speaking through puppets is less intimidating for many young students and thus results in a better oral presentation.

- Create a living tableau.

   Arrange children into an interesting frozen picture depicting any scene from a story, song, poem, or any other component of their studies, such as a pioneer family (Grade 4 Social Studies) or a scene from China (Grade 6 Social Studies). Play music or have a narrator read the poem, story synopsis, or a description of the scene. Then individual children can "come to life" and speak their thoughts to the audience. This idea is adapted from the drama technique called "inner dialogue." Costumes add interest.

Effortless Art Lessons

Here is a list of ten quick and simple art ideas, all of which can be done right in the classroom with only paper, pencils, and pencil crayons. Some of the suggestions may seem too simple for older students, but when creativity is encouraged, even Junior High students love them. The bonus is that the finished products make delightful wall displays, or can prompt writing assignments where students analyze or explain their creations. Enjoy!

People Pictures

• Finger People

Let children trace around their hands, then make each finger into a "finger person," complete with hair, hat, arms, etc. They can name their people.

• Wonderful Windows

What's behind a window? All children want to know. Have them draw no more than four different-sized rectangles on the page. They can trace or use geometry sets, or draw freehand. (For very young children, a photocopied page of empty rectangles is helpful.) They should decorate each window differently, showing curtains, people, pets, flowers, etc. Children can even tell stories through the windows.

• Shape People

Ask students to draw several different, large shapes, such as circles or triangles. Each shape becomes a different person, complete with features, arms and legs, hats, and names. Encourage older students to come up with alliterative names, such as Tearful Triangle or Sandwich Lover Square.

• Action Figures

This activity is fun because it involves "models." Select one or two students to "pose" in any action stance, and have others scribble the pose. Because the poses are scribbled, there is less concern about not being a "good drawer." Change models often. Since it takes only about five minutes to scribble a pose, many different poses can fill a single page.

Abstract Images

• Scribble Abstract
Invite children to doodle and scribble over an entire page (encourage minimum scribbling as opposed to filling in all the spaces). Then with crayons, they either color the "negative spaces" (holes between the scribbles), *or* try to find a shape to color hidden within their scribbles. Alternative: Have them scribble with their weaker hands. It's amazing what they come up with!

• Lines upon Lines
Have students draw as many different kinds of lines on the page as possible. Expect to see lines that are dotted, heavy, thick, thin, jagged, broken, and more. Lines should intersect and eventually cover the entire page. With one color only, students then highlight their favorite line, ready to justify their choice.

• Inside Out Abstracts
Invite students to draw simple, recognizable shapes from around the room, for example, pencils, chairs, plants, cushions, and books. Shapes should not all be rectangular and should overlap. Then, using either just pencil or crayons, students fill in the "negative spaces" where objects overlap. The finished products can be quite intriguing.

• Disappearing Hands
It's fun for students to trace their own hands. Similar to "Inside Out Abstracts," this lesson involves tracing the hand three or four times, turning the paper around, and overlapping the hands. Then the overlapping small shapes are all colored differently. Sometimes, it's hard to see the original hands in the finished product.

• Finger Bouquets
Children will enjoy the creativity here. They trace fingers, but not thumbs, several times, so that all fingers point upward. (Overlapping is good too.) Each finger is then topped with a colorful flower head. Instant bouquet!

• Simply Symmetry
Have students fold a page in half lengthwise. Then invite them to draw lines or simple images on one side, pressing heavily on the pencil. By flipping the page over, they can then see through the paper and trace the original drawing, creating an exact mirror image. Students can color the images either symmetrically or differently. They are delighted with the results.

6

Promoting Efficient
Classroom Practice

You have a job to do. Teaching. And you are a teacher because teaching is what you love to do. However, when you have so many daily routines and mandatory obligations to fulfill, sometimes getting down to teaching curriculum seems almost impossible. Any methods to streamline some of these procedures, or to lighten the workload somewhat, will result in more time being available for planning, talking with children, and providing personal guidance to individuals.

There are ways to lighten the workload, to simplify everyday actions, to make particular activities, such as dealing with marking or undone homework, less time consuming. These activities are all necessary, but sometimes handling them becomes more important than the teaching component they represent.

How many times have you thought that if you didn't have to track down undone homework so much, you'd have considerably more time? Or, if you could mark faster you could better plan the next day's lesson? These are common concerns for teachers. This chapter offers tips to help you deal with them, at least to some degree. By doing so you can free up precious time for more child-centred pursuits.

Similarly, the area of evaluation can consume enormous amounts of time. Although it is not my intention to go into great detail about assessment, I will make suggestions for authentic and performance assessment. As you know, I'm sure, these are the assessment techniques of the day, seen as the most beneficial, realistic, and empathetic forms of student evaluation. A list of helpful hints for their use has been included.

Finally, the huge issue of standardized testing remains, so it is in the best interests of everyone for students to be prepared for such testing. You know that trying to get a class to study or review material is frustrating. However, if the students can somehow be hooked into the task, review becomes time well spent. This chapter offers techniques, many of them both entertaining and content related, to use to facilitate the review process.

Ways to Organize Yourself and Your Class

Slow and steady is not always the best—especially if you are a teacher. Here are hints for streamlining basic classroom procedures.

• Be firm about filing.

Label colored file folders (Science IN; Science OUT) and keep them in a specific place. Train your students to hand everything in *only* in the correct folder. Once marked, you place assignments in the appropriate OUT folder. It's easy to grab a folder to take home for marking, and students learn responsibility for their work. Refuse to accept work anywhere else.

• Play the name game.

Keep a class list on your desk or pinned to your bulletin board for emergencies. (You won't waste time looking for one.)

• Keep a laminated, blank seating plan on or near your desk.

You can write on the plan with washable pen and make changes instantly.

• Be the early bird always.

Arrive early, not late, in the mornings. It's true that the teachers who arrive early are the best organized. Even 15 minutes makes a difference.

• Plan ahead.

Do your homework and make plans. Even sketchy plans are better than none. The best teachers—the ones who can spend the most time with their students—are those who plan ahead.

• Use a daily agenda.

Write on the board, in point form, what is going to happen each day. It is a visible check for you and your students, saving you from the constant "What are we going to do in …?"

• Start each day exactly the same way.

This consistency saves time and sets the tone for a comfortable day. (However, you don't have to maintain this approach all day: flexibility and spontaneity are key factors in motivation.)

• Use attention cues.

Don't begin talking until you can see the whites of their eyes. Establish and use consistently an attention cue, as suggested in Chapter 4.

• Watch your speaking speed.

Speak at a brisk pace. Surprisingly, a slow, steady voice, such as many primary grade teachers use, is not necessarily the best. Children respond better to a brisk presentation. In return, you can expect them to adopt a no-nonsense, efficient approach to their work.

- Give directions clearly.

  Be sure every student knows what to do. (See "Avoiding the Time-After-Time Ordeal," page 91.)

- Track students' movement through a sign-out sheet.

  Post a clipboard or piece of heavy cardboard near the door, with an attached pencil. If students leave the room for any reason, have them sign the sheet, indicate where they are going, and check off when they return. This practice saves teacher time and encourages student accountability, responsibility, and sense of importance.

- Teach "down time" strategies.

  Always tell your students what to do when they are finished assigned work. "Free time" too readily becomes wasted time. Give them two or three activity choices, for example, reading, drawing, or using the Fun Box (see page 29). Review expectations before every independent work activity.

- Design an emergency measures drawer.

  Prepare for the terrible day, that day when the class is too wound up to work and things seem to go from bad to worse. Stock a special drawer (or box or bag) with inexpensive, tangible treats that you can draw out at a moment's notice to reinforce positive behaviors. Use the treats as rewards for work, attention, and game winners. They will help you get the students back on track. Sometimes, these treats can mean the difference between a good day and a bad day. Just keep the supply well stocked, and don't allow students access to it—ever!

- Cast your net for volunteer help.

  Beyond parents (see Chapter 7), consider finding volunteers among unemployed people in the neighborhood; older students who have "spares" at school; seniors, perhaps from a nearby lodge; and your own students.

The Subject of Seating: Where Do I Sit?

Where to sit students in a classroom is always a dilemma. Should the independent workers sit at the back? Is it necessary to have the troublemakers close to your desk? There are as many different thoughts on these issues as there are teachers; however, a few ideas have worked well for my peers and me. Keep in mind, though, that students like having their own, familiar desks; it meets a need for order, structure, even security. So, once you decide on a seating arrangement, keep it for a reasonable length of time, such as a month or six weeks.

General Considerations

• Let the students choose.
On the first day of school, let students choose their own seats. Where they sit, beside whom, gives you important information about them. In addition, this choose-your-own-seat routine allows you time to get to know them a little, before enforcing your own plan.

• Elicit information about student preferences.
During the first week, either have students fill in a brief questionnaire (page 90) or have a quick mini-conference with each student where you ask the questions yourself.

• Encourage student flexibility.
Having said the above, any seating plan must also be flexible. From day one, make sure that students are aware that you control the room, that no one "owns" a particular desk or seat, and that you can, and will, make changes as necessary.

• Consider your ease of movement.
Do not seat a student who needs a lot of support in a difficult-to-reach area of the classroom. You need to be able to move freely around every student.

• Think clockwork rotation.
One interesting method of altering a seating plan is to number the seats in a sequential manner, then, on a preset day, for example, every Friday, students move one spot, maybe from seat 5 to seat 6, so that they are actually rotating around the room and everyone has equal time everywhere. Select a few desks to remain unnumbered for students with special needs. To prevent these children from feeling uncomfortable about remaining in the same desks, assure them they have "special" places.

• Appreciate that hard workers need time near you too.
Avoid the temptation to place all the conscientious, focused students at the back or much away from you. It's too easy to forget that they need, and deserve, equal time from you. A flexible seating plan should allow them their "time at the front" too.

Special Considerations

- Place students with visual or hearing deficits close to the front.
  This should be the first consideration when constructing a seating plan.

- Think "bad at the back."
  Seating the troublemakers and attention seekers at the back of the room means that fewer students will see their acting-out behaviors. If they're at the front, the entire class will be disrupted every time someone makes a face or falls out of a chair.

- Recognize that size matters.
  It's common sense that a taller student shouldn't sit in front of a smaller student, but sometimes even the most conscientious teacher forgets this. Think about yourself sitting behind that tall guy in the theatre …

- Be aware of friends and enemies.
  There is no point in putting students who dislike each other together. Doing so is just asking for trouble. Instead, allow the students the courtesy of sitting apart. You wouldn't choose to sit at a meeting beside someone you didn't care for. Similarly, if good friends tend to talk a lot, it may not be wise to place them together. Explain to them that they have all the rest of the time, outside class, to be together.

- Place distractible students strategically.
  Students who are more easily distracted than others should be seated towards the walls, and away from windows or busy areas. It's a misconception that seating such students near the teacher's desk is effective. Consider how much action goes on near your desk. There may be a better spot.

- Recognize good work buddies.
  If a couple of students work well together, keep them together. It is not viable to separate good work buddies just for variety's sake, although you may wish to do this for specific projects or classes. Similarly, don't always place a weak student beside a strong one, assuming that the strong will tutor the weak. Doing this may be useful at times, but the strong student needs the stimulation of an equally strong peer. Be flexible!

Seating Plans: Student Worksheet

1. Where do you like to sit in a classroom?

2. Why do you prefer that spot?

3. Is there anyone you really do not want to sit beside. If so, why?

4. Where did you sit in your class last year?

5. Can you see the board well?

6. Do little things bother you in class? Give examples.

7. Where do you really hate sitting in the room?

Avoiding the Time-After-Time Ordeal: Giving Clear Directions

There's not a teacher in the world who hasn't heard the infamous "What are we supposed to do again?" This question usually follows right after the directions have been given and is often echoed by several others in the room. The following sequenced list may seem redundant, foolish, or time wasteful, but unless everyone knows what to do, you will have a cacophony of confusion that is both time consuming and annoying to deal with.

1. Use your chosen attention cue first (see Chapter 4).

2. State that you are about to give directions and that everyone should look at you.

3. Provide the directions as simply as possible (point form) in more than one modality—auditory and written.

4. Immediately ask students to repeat back what they are to do.

5. Have several different students state the directions in their own words, being sure that they get the sequence of event correct. Provide clues like *first, then …*

6. If necessary, ask one more time, "What is the first thing you will do when I give you the start signal?"

7. Tell students what to do when they are finished the work. For example, tell them where to put completed work, to read, to use the Fun Box, or to do whatever you would prefer.

8. Give the start signal.

9. Go directly to any specific students who tend to miss the directions (perhaps students with special needs) and whisper to them, checking to see whether they know what to do. Be careful not to embarrass them with the attention.

10. Immediately reinforce how students have specifically followed the directions. "Good. You have all opened to page 45 and are beginning to read."

Defeating the Homework Demon: Handling It with Ease

Incomplete work or undone homework causes headaches for all teachers. Although parental involvement comes into play with the homework issue, there are a few tactics that even the busiest of teachers can employ to help deal with the problem.

Remember these two points:
1. You cannot force a student to work.
2. Whatever approach is used, there must be some connection between it and the undone work. Consequences should be logical and rational.

Proactive Measures

• Make homework meaningful.
If it is just "practice," say so. If it is to "put what you have just learned into a different context," let them know. If it is an extension of in-class learning, students will accept that. What they do *not* accept as easily is homework just for the sake of homework.

• Increase accountability.
Students need to know the importance of their work. Assure them that the work will be *marked* and/or *shared* (with parents, principal, or peers). Otherwise, students will tend not to finish the work or do it at all.

• Institute a system of homework buddies.
Use peer pressure to your advantage and create "homework buddies." Introduce the system by explaining its advantages and telling the class that everyone will be assigned a buddy by you. Buddies will work together for two weeks, then will be changed, so that everyone is buddy with everyone else by the end of the year.

What Buddies Can Do:
1. Buddies can phone or e-mail each other about homework to be done.
2. Buddies assume some responsibility for each others' homework. (You might give points if both buddies have finished their homework.)
3. Buddies can act for each other, initialling when work is put in the correct folder.
4. When one buddy is absent, the other can be responsible for collecting and returning homework.

• Teach good homework practices.
Students often don't know how to tackle homework. (See page 124.)

• Use an In checklist.
You need to know where finished work is. Attach a class list to the In folder and when a piece of work is handed in, initial the list, have the student do it, or call for both your initials and the student's.

Homework Checks and Consequences

• Send monthly homework letters.

Children work harder when their parents are kept informed. Once a month send home a computer print-out or brief note to all your students' homes, indicating done and undone work. This serves as a check for problem students as well as positive reinforcement for students who are finishing their work. Since you may not have time to compile these letters, assign this responsibility to an older student, a parent helper, or a volunteer senior.

1. Preserve the confidentiality of individuals by using numbers on the letters. You can add the names at the end.
2. Mail the first letter, along with a note to watch for further letters, on the last Friday of each month. Conscientious parents will then encourage their children to provide the letters.

• Create homework contracts.

Some students work well when under a contract. Although using contracts to encourage students to do their work has been overdone and criticized over the years, it remains a useable tool for *some* students. Students, with their parents, can fill in the rewards and consequences on the form.

• Set a time-out for homework completion.

When a student doesn't have work done, send him out of the room to a pre-designated area to complete the homework. The student cannot return to the classroom till it is done. The amount of time taken must then be paid back in some sort of after-hours tasks. Otherwise, the consequence is not specific to the idea of time lost when out of class. As long as you've checked with your colleagues, you might send students to a neighbor's class, the office, the school library, or a desk placed in the hallway right outside your door.

• Establish an after-school homework room.

Avoid referring to this opportunity for students to complete undone work under supervision as a detention. You can always find marking or planning to do for a half hour or so, while a student "catches up." Institute a duration policy whereby any student coming to the homework room must stay for at least half an hour. Otherwise, students may be tempted to complete work too rapidly. See if you can share the overseeing of this room with other teachers, parent volunteers, or seniors.

Homework Contracts: Rewards and Consequences

In order for a homework contract to be successful, rewards and consequences should be a shared responsibility of the parents and the teacher, and should be logical, manageable, and consistently delivered. Students need to be aware of the results of homework completion or incompletion, both at home and at school. Lines of communication should be kept open through phone calls, e-mail or a homework book, so that all the parties involved know what action has been or might be taken.

Possible Rewards

Additional time at home
- before curfew
- for TV
- in bed
- on computer

Additional allowance

Freedom from doing homework on specified days
- week night
- weekend

Special excursion with parent(s)
- day out
- night out
- holiday weekend

Special rights at school
- opportunity to work in library
- opportunity to work in the office, answering the phone, for example
- extra computer time
- opportunity to help younger students
- opportunity to be "first" in line, for games or for other pleasurable activities

Special time with teacher ("lunch")

Obviously, there has to be a good rapport between student and teacher for this to be seen as a reward.

Possible Consequences

- Extended homework period/night
- Loss of privileges, such as TV time
- Reduction in allowance

Note: Removal of privileges such as participation in team sports should be avoided if possible as these activities are desirable for healthy child development.

Homework Contract

For

_____

I agree to complete _____% of my homework for the (week/month) of _____.

If all my homework is done and handed in on time, I will be allowed to _____

_____

_____

If I do not live up to my end of the bargain, then I am prepared to _____

_____

_____

Student Signature _____

Parent Signature _____

Teacher Signature _____

Date _____

Managing All That Marking

Good teachers have lots of marking, which can become the straw that breaks your back. The following suggestions may help to lighten the load.

• Stagger written assignments.
Plan lessons such that those requiring written responses, and hence heavy marking, are not on adjacent days.

• Spot check.
Sometimes, mark only random parts of an assignment, perhaps certain questions, or the first and last paragraphs only. Students do not have to know when spot checking will occur. Even these checks can provide fairly accurate information.

• Initial completed work—and check off the names accordingly.
Obviously, this method does not provide feedback other than who has or has not done the work, but it can be a useful tool when you lack time for detailed marking.

• Do specific spot checks.
Mark specific sections of an assignment, while giving a general glance at the rest of it. Usually students are told ahead of time exactly what is being marked. For example, you might tell them that you are marking a writing assignment just for sentence structure.

• Scan the work quickly.
Once you "eyeball" a student's work, give a general mark, usually in multiples of five or ten. No specific comments need be given. Although you shouldn't rely on this method, as too many errors can be missed, it will speed up the marking process.

• Capitalize on four-phase marking.
This technique is useful for big assignments with an inherent subjective content, such as research projects, long pieces of writing, visual representations, science labs, and portfolios.
   a. *Phase 1:* Separate the assignments into three piles or groups—low, average, and high—by doing a quick scan. (These groups are not static.)
   b. *Phase 2:* Further divide the average (and most probably the largest) group into two piles, lower and higher, once again using the scan method. You now have four groups.
   c. *Phase 3:* Starting with the high average group, check each assignment quickly for previously identified key points or indicators. Look for about three to five of these indicators. Use a checklist, and simply check if the required indicators are present. You will gain a fair idea of what to expect of a good average assignment. Use the same checklist for the other groups. At this time, some papers may be shifted from one group to another. Marking can be finished after this stage, if necessary, by your assigning a "global grade" (one in multiples of 5 or even 10).
   d. *Phase 4:* Time allowing, do a complete, detailed reading and assign a more individual grade. Amazingly, most teachers will find that the score awarded after this phase varies only slightly from that awarded after Phase 3.

Sources of Help with Marking

Sometimes you need help to stay on top of the marking. Volunteers and students can be valuable marking assistants as long as you provide them with the necessary guidelines and take into account the type of assignment and how it will be marked. For example, you wouldn't expect a volunteer or a student to spot check or to mark a written paper.

- Use student markers.
  Consider having a few students help with marking after school or at noon. Doing so is useful if the following considerations are met:
  - There is an easily followed rubric *or* questions are T/F, multiple choice, or short answer.
  - Marking is a voluntary responsibility, not a punishment.
  - For confidentiality on select assignments such as tests, the work shows pre-assigned numbers rather than names.

  This practice works well when older students are asked to mark younger students' work. Sometimes when the "worst" or "shy" students are chosen to help, their self-esteem is given a boost and teacher-student rapport (one-on-one time with the teacher) increases.

- Solicit parent partners.
  As long as the parents have a good key and/or rubric, confidential tests or papers are "numbered," and the assignment is not one you want to use for assessment purposes, they make competent and enthusiastic markers. (See Chapter 7.)

- Use peer markers.
  In-class peer marking of work is an overused practice; however, it can be effective if you consider the following.
  - No names should appear on papers if there is a chance of prejudicing the markers, or if the papers are tests. (Refer to Freedom of Information and Protection of Privacy Act.)
  - Accountability is bumped up by markers putting their names on the papers they are marking.
  - Markers should learn something while marking. For example, they can be asked why a specific answer is correct or incorrect or what other responses might be correct. Without this dimension, peer marking is simply busywork.
  - Let students mark in pairs (each pair can mark two papers). Students will more likely catch marking errors and can discuss the answers together.
  - Ask markers to provide correct answers. Unless you want students to do corrections as an additional assignment, it is a good idea for markers to put in correct answers. Doing so serves as review and encourages additional learning.
  - Don't overuse the practice of students-as-markers. As appealing as peer marking may be, it can be a waste of time for many students. Use it sparingly, and consciously try to make it a learning experience by questioning and pointing out key concepts as you go.

More Than Just "Doing" the Marking—Handling It Well

You know how to mark; you also know that the process can be tedious and time consuming. Consequently, it is possible to forget the basics. I have found that keeping the following list handy lightens the load by keeping tips fresh in my mind.

- Make extra copies of mark sheets.
  Do this even if (especially if?) marks are recorded on computer. Keep the mark sheets in separate places. A sheet of lost marks is a teacher's nightmare!

- Read students' names last.
  Don't read the name on an assignment first. It creates a mental mark before you even look at the work.

- Say it on a stamp.
  If you find you're always writing the same comment on work, consider getting a stamp made at a copy shop or stationery store.

- Forget the red.
  Write on students' work with pencil rather than red pen. Pencil or erasable pen is much less invasive (especially after a student has poured her heart and soul into a piece of writing). Also, students can erase the comments should they decide to keep the writing.

- Make your comments stick.
  Writing comments on little "stick-ons" is less invasive; these are easily removed.

- Give two marks.
  Consider providing two marks on some assignments: one for the standardized mark (compared to peers), and one for the "improvement" mark.

- Make specific comments.
  Specific comments are more valuable than general ones. Instead of "Good work!" write, "You used capitalization well."

- Tell students what you will look for in future assignments.
  "I will look for the use of figures of speech." "I will look for use of the correct formula for the area of a triangle." Jot down what you told the class or student you would look for, so that you won't forget to do this.

- Don't be afraid to ask for more.
  If an assignment is far below expectations for a student, ask for a "redo." Accepting less than what the student is capable of lowers standards.

- Always reward.
  Use positive reinforcement consistently and don't overlook the appeal of tangible rewards, such as edibles, or visible rewards, such as colorful stickers, at *any* age!

Alternative Ways to Evaluate

You will be familiar with norm-referenced and criterion-referenced tests. Here is a list of other possible ways to evaluate students. These ways will not only make the evaluation process less stressful for the students (thus promoting a healthy class environment), but will give you a better picture of the whole child. Of course, not all ways work well with all students. Choose wisely.

• Informal Observations
Look for time on task, cooperation in groups, effort, listening skills, questioning techniques, work completion record, and general attentiveness. Combine your observations with anecdotal notes.

• Mastery Learning
Encourage students to work on their own to master a task, then report back to you when they feel they have done so.

• Written Responses
Ask for essays, critiques, summaries, and written evidence of the main ideas or most important components of a topic or issue. These types of tasks allow the students to record their individual thoughts and ideas. Evaluate the substance of the writing, as opposed to the form.

• Oral Responses One-on-One
Talk to your students individually to ascertain what they know. Doing this is time consuming, so use only as needed, perhaps with students who have special needs.

• Group-Recorded Responses
Children like this technique where they are broken into small groups and expected to discuss a topic, while being tape-recorded. Later, you can listen to their tapes for specific criteria that you established. Tell students ahead of time what kinds of responses you will be looking for.

• Technology-Based Chat Rooms
This technique is a favorite with students in grades 6 to 9. After groups of four or five have practised working in chat rooms (set up ahead of time), each student, seated at a computer, silently reads a hard copy of a poem, story, or article, chosen by you. Everyone in the class reads the same selection which allows for consistency among groups. After a pre-set amount of time, usually about 10 minutes, students log on and in chat room format, discuss the reading, based on criteria that you have previously established. They both ask and respond to questions about the reading. For example, one student may ask, "Does anyone understand the theme?" Another may reply, "I think it is about good versus evil." You get the hard copy of their chats. Amazing insights into your students can be gained from these.

- Need-to-Know Self-Evaluations

Older students in grades 5 to 9 establish the content of their evaluation by determining just what they need to know for a required project or subject. For example, Grade 7 students are told what they need to know about "writing labs" before entering Grade 8 Science. Each student then lists what she doesn't know, researches the list, and then is tested on that by a volunteer, peer, or parent.

- Portfolios

These allow for generalized evaluations. (A student handout on portfolios is included in Chapter 8.)

- Interviews

If time permits, conducting a brief interview, or conference, with each student, where you ask the student for a self-evaluation in a particular area, can be both informative and interesting. Sometimes, a student will see areas of both strength and weakness that you may have missed. Together you can come to an agreement on the actual mark, as well as on areas for improvement.

- Ongoing Journals

If a student has regularly written in a journal for a particular subject, a quick scan of its contents can provide some insights into the student's progress. However, for this approach to be effective, you must encourage honest expression of difficulties and accomplishments. A Math journal, where the student daily writes a brief note about what he did or did not understand, is a good example.

- Performance Tasks

When it comes to authentic teaching, these are the best. Performance tasks involve a product, a presentation, or a final outcome of some sort. They require students to do such things as research, gather, collate, problem-solve, report, write, summarize, design, integrate, present, synthesize, and evaluate.

Questions to Ask Yourself About Performance Tasks

It is not my intention to discuss the pros and cons of performance testing as opposed to criterion- or norm-referenced testing. However, I would like to suggest that these types of testing supplement each other. Here I am offering questions for you to ask yourself when calling for a performance task. If you answer such questions before students begin to work on a task, you can be confident that the task will permit effective performance assessment.

• What skills, knowledge, and attitudes do I want to test?

• How do these fit with the curriculum as well as with my long-term goals?

• What performance, activity, or product will best allow me to see how well students have developed the desired skills, knowledge, and attitudes?

• How well does this activity cross various disciplines (subject areas)?

• How authentic, challenging, and motivating is the task?

• How will I group the students for the most effective products?

• How long will I give them for completion? (Usually one week is sufficient.)

• How will I present the task in a motivating manner so as to hook them?

• What specific directions will I supply so that students can do the work as independently as possible?

• What materials will I give them? What will they need to find themselves?

• How will I evaluate? What specific criteria will I expect and be able to share with the students before they begin?

• What will individuals do at the end, to show independent learning?

Types of Performance Task Activities

Each of these tasks will require several different actions, such as gathering information, planning, collecting materials, and preparing of a final product. In addition, each task will enable you to test the knowledge, skills, and attitudes from different content areas. Some of the tasks, for example, researching and constructing, may be combined as necessary.

- Construct.
  Invite the students to build a structure of some sort—house, chair, bridge, boat, teepee—and present it.

- Research.
  Have the students research a topic in as many different ways as possible, then write and present a report, using visual aids.

- Interview.
  Teach the students how to conduct interviews and use questionnaires to determine public opinion and learn facts. Provide an assignment that requires the students to use these skills, then collate the information and present it in some way.

- Write.
  Choose any of the following writing tasks for your class to do as a whole, in small groups, or individually.
  - Write a class newspaper.
  - Write a collection of poems (after researching), and combine them into an illustrated book. One or two student-written poems can complete the anthology.
  - Write a skit or parody based on a famous story or nursery rhyme, and present the new version by acting it out.

- Create.
  Choose any of the following creative tasks for your students to work on individually or in pairs.
  - Create books for specific audiences, for example, Kindergarten children and seniors who have poor sight. Research topics, write, illustrate, put the package together, and present the finished book to the target audience.
  - Create a Web page, either personal or for the school.
  - Create an advertisement and videotape it for public viewing.

- Design.
  Invite your students, in pairs or small groups, to become involved in one or more of the following design tasks.
  - Design an exercise routine for a specific audience after researching their needs, the essentials of exercise, and so on. Use the program with the audience, for example, a Kindergarten class.
  - Design puppets and write and present a puppet show.
  - Design a dance routine for a specific audience. Present.

- Collate.

  Invite students to start a collection related to a curriculum topic of study. They can collect specific items for classification purposes, for example, pieces of fabric when studying texture in Science. Students should collate them according to criteria established either by you or through personal research, and present on a poster. Other examples of collectibles include leaves, small rocks, or dried food samples.

- Generate.

  Have your students generate an itinerary and route plan, using a map, for a real or imaginary journey.

- Collaborate.

  Introduce the concept of what makes an entrepreneur. Have students collaborate with peers to establish a small business, complete with advertising, cost factors, budget, and hours of operation. Possibilities include a lemonade stand, babysitting service, lawn-cutting services, and dog walking services.

- Teach.

  Once you have a working relationship with a teacher of a preferably younger grade, introduce the students, pairing them up with students from the younger grade. Invite your students to create lessons, such as in Art or Physical Education, for their buddies. After you have checked the lessons, your students could actually teach them to the younger students. Lessons in core subjects can benefit both groups.

De-stressing the Test: Six Ways to Study Vocabulary

Since many questions on standardized tests relate directly to the vocabulary of the course, studying vocabulary is important. Children loves games, so these activities will appeal to them.

• Word Lotto
  1. Students divide pages into nine parts (like X's and O's).
  2. From a list of vocabulary words, they select nine that are giving them trouble and write one word in each space.
  3. You read off the *definitions* of words, one at a time.
  4. Students cross off the appropriate words if they have them on their game boards.
  5. Prizes? If necessary provide small, tangible rewards such as candies.

• No-Stress Vocabulary Bee
  1. Have students form groups of three or four.
  2. Provide either definitions or words.
  3. Determine ahead of time how you want groups to respond. Options:
  • Groups write accompanying word or definition in allotted time. (The group with the most correct wins).
  • They raise their hands as soon as they think they know the correct answer. (There are points for the first correct response; for a tie, share the points.)
  • One group at a time answers, with words or definitions pulled randomly from a hat. Group members take turns answering, using the one-chance-to-ask-someone-else-in-the-group-for-help-if-necessary rule. There are points for correct responses.

• Crossword Puzzles
These are commonly used for vocabulary review, but as a change, have students create their own. Alternatively, check out Puzzlemaker.com.

• Vocabulary Doubles-Tennis
In pairs, students create lists of about ten words for which they know definitions. With another pair they "hit" words back and forth, allowing their opponents five seconds to come up with the correct definition. The students keep a record of points for correct responses.

Example: Pair 1 asks for the definition of *ecosystem*. Pair 2 gives correct response (one point), then asks for definition of *element*. Pair 1 can't define the term in given time (0 points), but moves on by asking for the next definition and so on. Pairs or groups can challenge each other.

• Vocabulary Stew
This activity involves both an awareness of word definitions, as well as an ability to use the words in context.

1. Write the words being studied on small slips of paper and place them all in one container.
2. Have students, in groups of about five, choose a Selector and a Speaker. (They may take turns.)
3. Each Selector chooses a word randomly and shows it to the entire class.
4. The group that pulled the word then has 20 seconds to create a sentence that illustrates an understanding of their word, or, in the case of primary students, to simply use the word in a good sentence.
5. The Speaker then presents the sentence. The rest of the class gives a thumbs up (good sentence that meets the criteria) or a thumbs down. As the teacher, you have the final say on whether the group gets one or two points for the sentence.
6. If the group cannot form a sentence in the given time, any other group that has a sentence ready for that particular word can go. If their sentence is good, an extra point is awarded to that group. This promotes thinking by all groups about all the words. If there is no sentence for the word, the next group selects a new word from the container.

Note: To make this activity more difficult, allow the group Selector to take two, or even three words at a time, all of which must fit into one sentence.

• Vocabulary Charades
A takeoff of the familiar charades game, this one involves the acting out of a vocabulary word on its own. Groups begin by selecting ten words from their notes for other groups to act. Actors cannot show how many syllables are in the word or what letter the word begins with. They act out either the action of the word or something that will make their peers think of the word. Follow charade rules. Allow 60 seconds maximum.

De-stressing the Test: Four Fantastic Strategies for Studying Content

Most standardized tests, other than those that directly focus on reading and comprehension, test subject content, so studying or reviewing of content is necessary. The following suggestions for in-class reviews seem to work.

- Double-Page Jot Notes
A blank page is folded in half vertically with key words on the left, and short, concise points on the right. Either side can be "covered" to allow studying. These double pages can be teacher or student made. Example:

Theme	*general underlying idea*
P of square	$s + s + s + s =$

- Ladders
Using a familiar format, students create their own Ladder questions by identifying key concepts and assigning points for each concept. (You can supply a list of concepts to be reviewed.) Then they "play the game" with each other to see who reaches 100 points (the top of the ladder) first. Ladders look like snakes with lines dissecting them. Each section of the ladder is worth 1 point. Game pieces (any small items, such as buttons or even squares of cardboard) are moved up the ladders. You could also have a backwards clause, where a completely wrong answer forces the student to go down the ladder. The game is very simple; the studying comes with the creation and answering of good questions. Example: Partner A asks B to explain metamorphosis (2 points); a correct answer allows B to climb two steps on the "ladder."

- RAP
RAP is the acronym for **R**ead, **A**sk, **P**araphrase. Students like this catchy acronym and so tend to remember it easily. They can RAP with a partner or alone, reading a selection or passage, asking questions (to self or partner) about it, and paraphrasing the reading.

- Mnemonics & Kid-Think
Whenever possible, use mnemonics—devices such as rhymes or formulas to aid the remembering of difficult concepts, ideas, definitions, or even spelling. Learning theory dictates that we learn by attaching new information to what we already know and understand. Keeping this in mind, put yourself into the shoes of your students, and try to see the new information from their viewpoints. Doing so usually makes it easier to create a useful mnemonic. By discussing the idea of using these helpful tricks and sharing them, the class can generate many themselves.

Example: In one class, students were having difficulty with the words protagonist and antagonist. They had recently created anti-smoking posters in Health. Using their understanding of the prefix *anti,* the teacher explained how the antagonist was *anti,* or *against,* the protagonist, just as anti-smoking is against smoking. After that, not one student confused the words.

Six Ways to Use Exemplars and Old Tests for Review

Reviewing from old tests is a common practice. However, many students find this so boring that they simply "tune out" and get nothing from the exercise. Familiarizing students with the format of tests, as well as the types of questions usually asked, is important, though. It behooves teachers to do the review in as interesting a manner as possible. The following suggestions have worked for me.

• Don't review an entire test at one sitting. Keep sessions to no more than 10 or 15 minutes at a time.

• Review in a "game" format. Play girls against boys to see who can answer the most correctly.

• Pretend it's a mini-test. Hand out small sheets of paper and have students do a few questions from the test. Mark together and award mini-prizes, such as candies and tokens, for top marks.

• Assign partners one page or section of the test each. Partners then prepare mini-lessons based on their sections. They present the concept or reading to the class and "teach" to the questions. When students do the reviewing, it seems much less boring to the rest of the class. Not all partners should present at one time or even on one day.

• Make overheads of sections of the test and work through the test with the overhead projector, using different colored pens to highlight key words, etc. For some reason, students attend more closely when a review is done in this fashion.

• Use questions from old tests for a Test Bee, where teams compete to provide the most correct answers. To avoid putting less capable students in a stressful position, have a "lifeline" rule, whereby they can ask one other person on their team for advice if they do not know an answer. Or, have the team choose a Shaman, the one individual to whom students can turn for advice.

7

Drawing on Volunteer Strength

Busy teachers are often strapped to find the time for tutoring after school, planning field trips, changing bulletin boards as often as they would like, listening to individuals read, and so on. Some teachers are fortunate enough to have full-time aides in their classrooms, but most are on their own.

Volunteers can be a valuable resource and way to extend teacher time. However, some studies report that teachers don't like having them in their classrooms. Although it's true that the presence of volunteers can require extra planning, such is not necessarily the case. Particularly with children in Grades 5 and below, parents can be wonderful helpers; they tend not to be as readily accepted by students in Grade 6 and up.

Parent volunteers (or any volunteers for that matter) can be amazingly useful in many ways. They can save you from busywork, such as filing, decorating, and photocopying, and free you to better foster the development of your students. Similarly, volunteers can tutor, share their own skills and expertise, and help in the classroom. The trick is in finding the right match between your classroom needs and the availability and strengths of potential volunteers.

Many parents have special skills or hobbies that could be of great interest to you and your class. Early in the year, a simple questionnaire, such as the one following, can provide you with this type of information. It can guide you when you need to solicit a parent volunteer. Similarly, the lists "A Dandy Double Whammy" and "Activities Where Parent Volunteers Are Great" should validate parents' desire to volunteer and help them choose areas of personal strength in which to work.

Sometimes, the parent will contact you and express a desire to help out. Even if you have yet to envision a need, it is important not to turn this parent off. Offer him something to do, even if it's not in your room. Perhaps the parent would be willing to give the office or another teacher assistance.

Using parent power effectively begins with an assessment of some of the types of parents in your class group, an awareness of how to deal most effectively with them, and an understanding that not all types can, or will, be of assistance to you. This book does not try to ascertain why parents behave the way they do, nor to take into account all the many responsibilities and concerns they have. Rather, it suggests a few characteristics of some of the different parent types and recommends which types may be more approachable for in-class assistance. In addition, although this chapter focuses on parents, the ideas and thoughts can, of course, be applied to any volunteers in the classroom.

First, consider the issue of communication between yourself and your students' parents, especially potential volunteers. One of the biggest problems experienced between home and school is poor communication. Whether or not you are hoping to have parent volunteers, you need to communicate regularly and efficiently with all parents; parents have a right to know how their children are doing and you will avoid later problems caused by poor communication. If, for example, parents have not been informed that their child is misbehaving, then suddenly get a "last chance" call, these parents will demand much of your time, and rightfully so, for detailed explanations. This chapter features a list of good ways to keep the lines of home and school communication open.

Then, once you have a prospective volunteer, you need to know just what you can expect from that person. A list of suggestions is included, along with tips for tutoring in both reading and writing, two areas in which parents frequently help.

Be sure to value your parent volunteers. They can contribute greatly to your ability to spend more quality time with your students.

Questionnaire for Parents

I am sure you have many strengths and interests, and I would greatly appreciate having an opportunity to learn what some of them are. Please respond to this questionnaire and return it with your child. If I can see a way in which your strengths and interests might benefit the class, I will see whether it is feasible for you to give us some help.

Are you interested in doing some volunteer work in the school? _____

If so, are there specific days/times when you would be available? _____

When? _____

Do you have any hobbies, skills, or interests that you think may be of use to us this year?
If so, please describe briefly.

_____

_____

Would you prefer to work with students directly, for example, as a tutor or group work helper, or to do such tasks as photocopying and filing?

_____

Do you have transportation so that you could get here quickly if necessary? _____

Have you taken a first aid course? _____

Would you be willing to accompany the class on a full-day or half-day field trip? _____

Would you be willing to do some volunteer work from your home (for example, organizing special events such as track and field days or fun fairs, typing, phoning, soliciting products for a silent auction)?

_____

If so, what type of option most appeals to you? _____

Please share any other comments or questions you have. _____

_____

_____

Where and when is the best time to contact you? _____

Thank you for taking the time to complete this form.

Looking at Parents as Potential Volunteers

The following are general guidelines to assist you in choosing which parents to approach or accept as volunteers. Remember that no parent can be forced into a single category, any more than a child can. Consider the categories kindly, and keep an open mind.

• The Overprotective Parent

This parent "rescues" and "saves" the child all the time. Help the child to become more independent, and never allow the overprotective parent to tutor her own child at school. Such a parent is good to ask for help, though, as she usually wants to be a part of her child's class.

• The Invisible Parent

Don't assume that the parent is invisible due to lack of caring. Consider possible causes such as illness, overwork, fear, and embarrassment, and treat with respect. Send little notes home regularly and phone often, even if just to leave a message. It's a waste of your time to approach this parent for volunteering.

• The Angry Parent

Listen carefully when such a parent speaks and check to see whether your perceptions of the child match. If they do not, tred lightly and keep the child's welfare in mind. Be supportive; do not provoke. Deal *at school* with problems you have with the child. Surprisingly, the angry parent might be a good choice to ask for in-class assistance. If he or she agrees to help, it can be a positive experience for everyone. However, ask politely, and do not try to persuade.

• The Defeated Parent

Such a parent has usually already heard many negative comments about the child, so try to remain positive, even when it is hard to do so. Remember that problems may not be due to parenting. Be empathetic. Find something positive about the child to share such as "Johnny is very creative." It might be worthwhile to solicit assistance from this parent, since he or she is seeking some way to interact with the student in a positive manner.

• The Single Parent

This parent is usually overworked and has virtually no free time. Also, if both parents in a split family approach you with different expectations, you may face problems. It is usually a poor idea to have either parent help in the classroom, unless there is obvious mutual cooperation between them.

• The Impossible-to-Get-Rid-of Parent

Such a parent is always at the school or on the phone. Don't judge and try not to become annoyed or frustrated. Instead, put her to work. She is a good parent to have as a volunteer, although not necessarily right in your room.

- The Know-It-All Parent

  Expect this parent to constantly make suggestions to you about your teaching, child management, and so on. Accept the suggestions graciously; you don't have to use them. The know-it-all parent usually makes a good volunteer; she can put all her wisdom to work.

- The Helpless Parent

  Sometimes you meet a parent who feels she can do nothing right—ever! Whether her child is doing poorly or well makes no difference. She sees herself as a failure. Tred gently. Be empathetic, but *don't* ask her to volunteer. You will spend more time coaching her than your students.

- The Cameo Parent

  This parent, although unable to commit to regular times in the classroom, is eager to assist whenever she can. Accept her offer and use her skills as an exciting guest speaker, perhaps on her field of work; an expert assistant for special tasks; or a "real-world" presenter of dramatic readings.

- The Work-at-Home Parent

  Some parents want to be involved with their students' school life, but are heavily absorbed by their own businesses which they operate from their homes. They may be willing to talk to your class about entrepreneurship, but more likely would prefer to do such work as researching topics, collating materials, and creating memos or letters for you from their homes.

- The Shy Parent

  Such a parent wants to help, but is overly shy and quiet around groups of children. For one-on-one tutoring, she may be ideal. This parent will be hesitant to approach you, so you will have to seek her assistance more openly.

- The Old Faithful Parent

  This wonderful parent is always there when you need assistance, never refuses your invitation to help out, and is, therefore, easy to take advantage of. Be careful not to overuse this person. Keep in mind that, although she is dependable, she has other commitments as well. It is a good idea to save this parent for situations when you are unable to solicit help elsewhere.

A Dandy Double Whammy:
Teachers Gain and Parents Gain When Parents Are in the Classroom

These benefits are presented from the parents' point of view.

• Time
Your assistance at school will give the teacher more time for planning, trying new strategies, and working directly with students.

• Help for Your Child
By playing the role that a paid aide would have played, finances permitting, you will help your child's teacher to help your child.

• Satisfaction
You will gain great personal satisfaction helping the students.

• Learning
When you work in school, the chances are great that you will learn new skills and be exposed to ideas that may be useful at home, as well as in the classroom.

• Support
The entire school, including the office and library, can benefit from parental support and consequently, will function more efficiently—a boon to your child.

• Communication
Lines of communication are kept open and students see that you are welcome at school. Parent-teacher support for students is strengthened.

• Strengths
If you have any special strengths, skills, or hobbies, you can serve as a guest speaker or instructor. What better way to share your strengths and add depth to the teacher's program?

• Discipline
The presence of another adult in the classroom encourages students, particularly young ones, to behave better, thus enhancing learning for all.

• Respect
By being a school volunteer, you are demonstrating your respect for education and for the teacher, something that is important for your child and others to realize.

Activities Where Parent Volunteers Are Great

Whenever parent volunteers can take over jobs that free up teacher time for more valuable pursuits or that enhance student learning, they are a real boon to the school. The following list of teacher-approved roles outlines specific ways in which potential volunteers might serve the classroom or school.

Supporting Roles

• Reading/Writing Buddies
Provide parents with copies of "Tips for Volunteers on Tutoring Reading" or "Tips for Volunteers on Tutoring Writing."

• Exam Proctors
Parents are vigilant watchers. Remember to tell them how much or how little help can be given.

• Markers and Recorders
Given a specific rubric to follow, or a simple exercise that has exact answers, parents make great markers. They can record marks too, although the Freedom of Information and Protection of Privacy Act may not allow this in your school. Check with your principal.

• Chief Communicators
Parents can serve as contact persons for your class and be responsible for letting other parents know about important activities, report cards, and interviews. If phone numbers are unavailable, these parents can arrange for other methods of communication, such as hand-delivered newsletters.

• Chaperones Extraordinaire
Some parents love to go on field trips with children. Their presence promotes safety and focused learning.

• Administrative Assistants
There are so many time-consuming clerical duties, such as checking attendance, filing, photocopying, and laminating, that steal a teacher's time from students. Let parents help here.

• Game Masters
A great way to use volunteers is to have them oversee games that reinforce skills. Many wonderful games are available, but usually the teacher has no time to monitor their use.

• Small Group Overseers
Parent volunteers can work with small groups in areas such as science experiments, art projects, and research projects.

Major Roles

• Changers of Bulletin Boards

If a volunteer is so inclined, provide materials, theme, and student work and let her tackle the bulletin board. I once had a parent volunteer who was an interior decorator. I would phone and tell her what my next theme was to be, and she would come totally prepared.

• Field Trip Planners

Although you must plan the field trip in accordance with your curriculum, once the destination has been established, you could have volunteers plan the details, writing letters to go home, arranging transportation, collecting fees, and so on.

• Interior Decorators

Some parents love to either help students make and hang seasonal decorations or create seasonal displays.

• Special Event Coordinators

All manner of special events, such as track and field days, drama productions, concerts, dances, parties, and carnivals, will benefit from the helping hands of parents. Beyond overseeing the event itself, volunteers can help plan and execute it. Give parents a brief written overview of what is needed, and trust their expertise.

• Out-of-Class Volunteers

Some parents want to volunteer, but are unable to come to the school. They can research information for upcoming themes (on the Internet, at libraries), collect resources, solicit sponsors for activities, or even supply the class with worthwhile "freebies." I once had a parent who desperately wanted to help out but worked full time in her own copy shop; she frequently sent colored paper samples to the class and did occasional laminating, coiling, etc. from her place of work.

• Special Speakers

A parent with a special skill or hobby, or even a vocation of interest, can make an excellent guest speaker. For example, I knew a nurse who often spoke to classes about hygiene and nutrition.

• Valuable Instructors

Some parents are very talented and are willing to share their talents with students in a class setting. For example, they might teach art or music lessons for the teacher who doesn't have that background.

How to Get Parent Volunteers Going

In the hectic day of a teacher there is little time for chat. Here are some suggestions for quick information exchange with volunteers to your classroom.

- Prepare the way for parents.
  Prepare students for parents' help by advising them of what is going on, who is coming, and how you expect them to behave.

- Don't keep the office in the dark.
  Be sure to let the principal know exactly what is going on. Provide her with a written synopsis of the volunteer's actions, if required. Tell the secretary, too, when a parent volunteer is expected. In one unfortunate incident, a male parent volunteer was escorted *out* of the building by a custodian who thought he was "up to no good." Don't let this embarrassing situation happen to you.

- Provide a parent package.
  As a general courtesy to parent volunteers, you might offer them a file folder with pertinent information, such as a class list, a school map, locations of washrooms, fire drill exits, names of principal, secretary, and custodian and so on. A number of folders can be prepared before the school year begins; a parent volunteer can make more folders as necessary.

- Be explicit in what you want volunteers to do.
  Be specific in your directions, explanations, and expectations. It is not good to approach parents with a vague idea of what you need or want done. Figure it out clearly first, then provide them with written directions, whether it's for one-on-one reading or field day planning. After the first time you've done it, this will be automatic, and you can recycle handouts prepared for your volunteers.

- Don't play hide and seek.
  Say where you will be; be available when you say you will be. Let the volunteers know if there are changes to the original plan.

- Watch the clock.
  Let parents know exactly how much time you will give to the project, and when, or if, you will be available to provide guidance. You might say, "Please read with Tommy in the library for 20 minutes."

- Mind your manners.
  Be polite and show appreciation for the help. Treat parent volunteers with respect. Remember that they are not paid or trained staff members, "gofers," or babysitters whose presence frees you to get a coffee.

- Follow up faithfully.
  Use school letterhead or thank-you notes to provide written appreciation. You do not have to do this every time a parent volunteers (unless it is a one-time occasion, such as a field trip), but certainly at the end of the year. Consider having students write the thank-you letters.

How to Achieve Good Communication with Parents

Keep the lines of communication open, no matter what obstacles you might face. The time needed for proactive communication is time well spent. The following suggestions have proved successful.

Sharing Information Visually

- Trust the mail.
  Mail home your first newsletter (or otherwise ensure its arrival). Tell parents when to expect the following newsletters to arrive home with the students, for example, the first Friday of every month. Newsletters serve as valuable lines of communication.

- Ask for signatures.
  Have a tear-off section on every newsletter for parents to sign and return. This is your check that the letter got home. Points or little rewards for students who return the signatures quickly work well.

- Write a letter of introduction.
  Have a personal letter introducing yourself to the parents ready to go home in the first week. (Avoid using a business letter; it is too cold and formal.) Consider including information such as where you received your university degree, what previous experience you have had, what your strengths are, and, of course, why you are looking forward to the upcoming year with their children. Keep the letter light and inviting.

- Be a persistent publisher.
  Write a brief monthly newsletter. If the school, as a whole, produces a newsletter, add your own page to the official letter. Here you can outline the latest units of study, in-class events, and so on. This is an excellent way to keep parents informed. They will know just what their children are doing in your class.

- Implement courier envelopes.
  Have every student decorate a large brown envelope in any way desired. This envelope then becomes the official bearer of newsletters home and signatures back. All envelopes are kept in a special place at school. Students become more conscious of not losing the envelopes; they feel a sense of ownership.

- Feature good news in your newsletter.
  Be sure to include accolades for specific accomplishments and samples of students' good work.

- Send special invitations.
  For all special events, such as concerts, assemblies, sports days, school carnivals, or any whole-school events, send written invitations to parents, either by mail, in the special envelopes, or hand-delivered by students. Include "free" tickets.

- Consider using agendas.

  Any book that goes back and forth between home and school and lists assignments to be done, due dates, undone work, and so on serves as an agenda and a direct form of communication between home and school. Both teachers and parents initial the books. This practice can save considerable time that might otherwise be spent chasing down undone work.

- Be a techie.

  If you have e-mail access at school, offer your e-mail address to parents as a method of contacting you. Allow a few minutes (when you have a volunteer, when students are doing busywork …) to review your e-mails daily. Don't let messages pile up, though; then you're not promoting communication.

Sharing Information Verbally

- Teacher, call home.

  Make it a practice to call all parents to welcome them to your room. Make the calls during the first week of school, or, better yet, before school begins in the fall. Doing so sets the tone for positive communication practices for the rest of the year. Make intermittent calls after that and not just when a problem arises.

- Open your door.

  Explain to parents orally or in writing your Open Door Policy. Parents are welcome in your class, but they must first let you know when they are coming.

- Conduct class meetings for parents.

  Early in the year, invite the parents of all the students in your class to a meeting (this can be tied to the school Open House if preferred), where you clearly explain your expectations, rules, long-term goals, etc. Thereafter, you might hold about two more class meetings to deal with common issues that concern parents. Phone parents to attend.

- Make Friday phone calls.

  If one or two students are having particular difficulties, either with the curriculum or with behaviors, make an arrangement to call the parents and update them on Fridays. Keep each conversation brief, no more than five minutes, and have anecdotal notes on hand when you call. The consistent home and school communication helps everyone.

- Let parents know when you are available.

  Some parents are uncomfortable with written communication and prefer to speak to you directly. To prevent a barrage of phone calls when you are not free to talk, establish a time when you can be reached by phone and be available then. A half hour per week is sufficient.

Smile—You're in a Parent-Teacher Interview!

For many teachers, the thought of parent-teacher interviews is, at best, uncomfortable. Think how it must be for the parents! The tension of this situation can be lessened if you are well prepared. The following suggestions may serve as last-minute reminders.

• Be on time.
Being prompt is both courteous and professional.

• Stick to the schedule.
Keep the interview to the allotted time. If you need more, set up another appointment.

• Be prepared.
Have marks, tests, student work samples, and records of assignments with you in a neat, organized folder.

• Be polite.

• Be diplomatic.
Remember that the student being discussed is the offspring of the adult(s) facing you.

• Remember why you're there—and stay on track.
Both you and the parent are there for one reason only—the student's welfare.

• If the student is present, talk *to* him, not *about* him.

• List behaviors.
Note any positive and negative behaviors of importance, including late arrivals, missed classes, and detentions. Be sure to write them down ahead of time.

• Discuss marks from two points of view.
Discuss marks "compared to the norm" (parents want to know this) and in terms of "personal improvement." Both aspects are important. Suggest whether or not you think the student is working to potential.

• Invite parental questions and comments.
Ask the parent what she would like to know, or if there are any aspects of the student's home life she would like you to be aware of.

• Make constructive suggestions.
Be prepared to offer specific suggestions for improvement, even with top students.

• Sum up what has been talked about and what decisions have been made.
Doing this enables all partners to be clear about where the student is currently and what direction is being taken for the future.

Tips for Volunteers on Tutoring Reading

As a volunteer, you want to help students read, but may not know where to begin. There is more to tutoring than just listening to a student read and correcting mistakes. Some students may be reluctant to read at all, especially if they have experienced failure in the past. Here is a sequence of steps that should simplify the tutoring of a reader of any age. In this outline, the student is a boy.

1. Begin gently.

   Reassure the student by conveying genuine interest and compassion. Saying a few words about something other than the reading helps.

2. Make sure you read first.

   To set the stage gently, read a short part of the selection to the student. Finger-point to the words as you read.

3. Ask the student what the problems are.

   The student will often tell you frankly what difficulties he is having. If he doesn't respond, ask him to read a little.

4. Prompt and cue.

   Provide help in the form of subtle cues when the student is stuck or makes an error. For example, rather than giving the whole word, give part of it. Avoid rescuing the student every time he makes a mistake.

5. Stop and start.

   Practise stopping after a sentence (or paragraph) and reviewing both the errors and the general meaning. Paraphrase the content if the student is unable to.

6. Take little steps.

   Keep going forward and back. For example, read three sentences, then go back and review the entire meaning; read a couple more, then go back to the beginning again. This forward-and-back movement improves comprehension.

7. Offer positive reinforcement constantly.

   Point out where the student is improving or showing strength. There is no such thing as too much positive reinforcement.

8. Review big chunks.

   After a couple of pages (or paragraphs, or, with a short story, the entire story), stop and review the entire reading so far. Ask specific content questions. If the student answers correctly, ask more abstract, or opinion type, questions. If he is unsure, either prompt or return to the text.

9. List recurring problems.

   Keep a running list of the most common errors or difficulties the student is having. You can review these later or share them with the teacher.

10. End on a high.

    Tell the student you enjoyed working with him and point out strengths you have observed.

Tips for Volunteers on Tutoring Writing

It is difficult to tutor writing, especially if you don't know how much the student can or is willing to do alone. Frequently, students who have had difficulty with writing projects will try to get you to do most of the organization and writing for them. The following points should help you to manage this situation more easily.

1. Being gently.
   Talk briefly about something other than writing; create a relaxed atmosphere.
2. Determine the writing task.
   Find out what the student is required to write, for example, sentence, paragraph, essay, story, letter, journal, or report.
3. Identify problem areas.
   Ask the student what she has difficulty with. Her response will guide your assistance; you'll have an idea where to begin. Usually a student will verbalize some idea such as "getting started" or "spelling."
4. Discuss the topic and type of writing.
   Talk together about the topic and product. Generate ideas together, being careful not to spoonfeed, that is, provide all the ideas. You can be the "recorder" who jots ideas down, if the student is a slow writer. Ask whether the student has any relevant notes or handouts about this form of writing. Use them if she does.
5. Organize ideas together.
   Ask how the ideas can be organized. If the student suggests something like webbing, go with that; any visual representation of the ideas that shows organization of thought will work. Don't suggest outlining at this point.
6. Help with the beginning.
   Discuss ways to get started. Most reluctant writers struggle with this aspect of writing so come up with ideas together, then let the student make a choice. Help her write the beginning whether it's one sentence or several paragraphs, or one good sentence; read it back before continuing.
7. Encourage independent work.
   Praise the beginning and gently encourage the student to continue on her own. If she is reluctant, work through a few more words, sentences, and paragraphs together. Focus on content rather than mechanics, such as spelling and grammar, stopping to reread after finishing small sections. In this way you will catch confusion early.
8. Discuss possible endings.
   Let the student choose the ending. Help her see why this ending will be good.
9. Proofread together.
   Have the student read the piece to you. If she stumbles, suggest underlining that part for reworking later. Help her to make the writing flow smoothly, offering advice as needed.
10. Check spelling and grammar together.
    Once the general gist of the writing is intact, go over it together for errors. Keep a list of the most common errors to share with the teacher or use for future reference. Provide lots of praise for the finished product.

8

Helping Students over the Hurdles

As every teacher knows, one of the biggest time wasters at school is having to repeat the same directions over and over again. Therefore, this chapter addresses some of the most common concerns that students have, so that they can proceed on their own. It features handouts for the students on such topics as

- doing homework
- studying for exams
- managing time
- writing tests
- organizing notes and assignments
- asking for help
- creating portfolios

These may seem like simple matters to you, but if you think back to all the time you have spent on them, I'm sure you'll agree that providing students with easily readable handouts is desirable. It also shows your compassion because you're helping students deal with issues that cause them anxiety. Doing so helps keep student-teacher rapport intact.

Homework Tips for Students

- **Use an agenda daily.**
  Every day record your homework or upcoming assignments or tests in an agenda or homework book. Use the book even if it's to write "no homework."

- **Pick a special place.**
  Always do your homework in the same place; your brain will expect you to do homework here.

- **Pick a special time.**
  Do homework at the same time every day. Again—train your brain! Choose at least a half hour daily if you are in grades 1 to 3, and up to one and a half hours for higher grades. Junior High students may require up to two hours a day. Allow yourself one day off a week for good behavior. Stick to it for the duration.

- **Stick to the pattern.**
  No homework? Use the same time and place to review earlier schoolwork. Keep that brain trained.

- **Refuse to be interrupted.**
  Don't let anything come between you and doing your homework during the set time. Put off phone calls, TV, home duties—whatever. Make sure everyone knows that this is your work time.

- **Treat homework like a job.**
  Actually, it *is* your job. Treat it seriously and the gains will be great.

- **Be prepared.**
  A few minutes before your assigned time, go to the bathroom, collect all necessary materials, get a drink, in other words, do whatever you have to, to get ready. Don't use assigned homework time for any of these activities.

- **Keep a record.**
  When doing homework, you may run across things or ideas you don't understand. Jot them down (don't rely only on your memory), and ask the teacher about them the next day.

- **Take the challenge.**
  Think of the homework as a contest—a challenge between yourself and the teacher. Declare yourself the winner by getting the work done quickly and correctly.

- **Reward yourself.**
  When you have successfully completed your set period of homework, give yourself a little reward, such as something special to eat or drink, or a phone call to a friend.

Studying Tips for Students

• Use your trained brain.
  Use the same-time-same-place routine you have developed for homework, but extend the time as necessary.

• Start studying early.
  Don't leave all your studying until the last night. Cramming will just give you a headache and doesn't help much with the tests.

• Go with a guide.
  If the teacher doesn't give you a study guide (most will if you ask for one), take the time to do a general review and write out what the main areas to be studied are. Use point form, then refer to this outline as you study. Use text headings to guide you.

• Keep it quiet.
  It seems obvious, but don't study in a noisy place. Find a place where you can focus. Some students find they can study better with music playing. If you're one of them, that's great, but if you start singing along with the tunes, you aren't studying.

• Break up the content and break up the time.
  Divide into small chunks the material you want to cover, and study one chunk at a time. Review that part before going on to another. Allow yourself breaks, too. After about a half hour, get up, stretch, and move around.

• Write the ideas out.
  For many ideas, concepts, and skills, you will find it a good idea to look at them on paper, then write them out from memory. The act of writing helps you to remember.

• Know those words.
  All tests, no matter what the subject is, expect you to know the vocabulary of the course. They may ask for it directly, as in "Define these words," or indirectly (hidden in the questions). So make a list of all the possible vocabulary and study it. Just knowing the vocabulary can improve your mark a lot.

• Use the RAP strategy.
  For long sections of notes or text, use RAP: **R**ead a short section (about one page). **A**sk yourself what you just read. **P**ut it in your own words. This way, if you are just reading and not remembering, you'll catch yourself at once.

Studying Tips for Students (*continued*)

• Do the two step.
For sections you must remember in more detail, like procedures, lists, or steps, take the two-steps-forward-one-step-back approach. Read a little bit, review it, then add the next part. Now go back and review both parts together. Go further. Now go back to the beginning and review it all. Keep studying like this until you have all the material covered.

• Create memory aids.
Make up little rhymes or sentences using the first letter of each word in a series, for example, **E**very **G**ood **B**oy **D**oes **F**ine for the lines on a treble musical staff. Or come up with words using the first letters of the key words, such as HOMES to recall the five Great Lakes. Use anything, no matter how silly, to help remember important facts.

• Have a study buddy.
Some people work better with a partner, but only do this if you know you will both work and be able to help each other. Study buddies should talk lots about facts relevant to the material to be covered.

• See it in your head.
Try to visualize or picture words and ideas in your head. Talk to yourself while you do this. You might even try to associate feelings with the information you're focusing on.

• Underline and highlight.
Underlining and highlighting really do work as long as you are careful not to mark everything. Stick to key points, vocabulary words, and the most important facts.

• Use graphic organizers.
As you are studying, organize the material in a visual way by clumping similar ideas into clusters, or webs, by mapping, outlining, or grouping points, by making comparison charts, and so on. Being able to see the information in a new light will help you to remember it.

• Skim and scan.
Instead of reading every word, skim. Do a quick survey of the chapter or section you are studying and pick out the headings, boldfaced words or phrases, and key points. Then, scan. Quickly read to locate specific points with which you feel unfamiliar.

Time Management Tips for Students

• Make a big calendar for your bedroom.
Keep the calendar up-to-date with all the things you have to do, including homework assignments, team activities, and special occasions. Check it each morning when you get up, and you'll never miss anything. Basically, plan your time at least a week in advance.

• Follow a routine.
Make it a habit to do homework, home duties and chores, and practice (such as for piano or dance) as close to the same time every day as possible. Doing so trains the brain to expect certain behaviors at this time, and learning is maximized. Such actions should become as habitual as brushing your teeth.

• Get enough sleep.
Plan for about eight hours of sleep a night. Getting this can be tough at times, but you'll feel better for it. Be especially careful before exams. Many students study until all hours, then are too tired to do their best.

• Hit the sack early.
If you practise going to bed at a reasonable hour on school nights, you'll be able to get up more refreshed in the morning.

• Don't overdo it.
Don't take on more activities than you can comfortably handle. If you're feeling stressed and tired and don't seem to have enough time for everything, give something up (no, not homework!). You have your whole life to do all these things. School is the most important right now.

• Take personal time.
Remember that you deserve some time for yourself. Be sure to budget for personal time so you can play with your dog, phone your friends, watch TV, go on the computer, or just be alone.

• Budget surfing time.
It is very easy to spend a lot of time at the computer. Allow yourself a certain amount of time only, and stick to it. Use an alarm clock to remind you when the time is up, and stop when it goes off. The computer is, perhaps, the biggest time gobbler for young people today. Be aware of this.

• Plan for exercise.
Unless you are actively involved in a sport or other physical activity, be sure to plan some exercise time. Even a brisk walk outside will do. A little exercise every day will help you to think and react more quickly.

• Ask for help if you're overloaded.
It's OK to ask for help from family members or peers if you take on more than you can handle. They cannot do your homework for you, but there are times when others can help with such activities as home duties, walking the dog, or cutting out pictures for a project. You are human. There is only so much you can do. If you can't get everything done, say so, and let others pitch in.

Test Writing Tips for Students

- Be on time.
  Being on time for a test makes you feel more ready and comfortable. When you know there is a test after recess, for example, don't dawdle when the bell rings or go to the washroom at the last minute. Arriving late by even just a few minutes, when others have already started, creates an unnecessary feeling of stress and anxiety.

- Have your tools ready.
  Be sure you have everything you need for the test ahead of time. A last-minute search for a calculator for a Math test or an eraser for a writing test will leave you feeling stressed-out before you begin. Find out if you can use pen or pencil, and be ready.

- Dress for the test.
  Yes, there is a right way to dress for a test. Wear comfortable clothes (tight pants will drive you crazy when you have to sit for a long while), and think "layers." You want to be able to take off something if you get too warm. Other than being too cold when writing a test, there is nothing worse than being too hot, because you will get sleepy.

- Drink water.
  If permitted, bring a water bottle to the test. Being even a little dehydrated reduces brain functioning. Also, sipping water helps to reduce the uncomfortable feeling sometimes experienced when a question makes you draw a blank.

- Forget other people and relax.
  Don't even look at anyone. Think of yourself as a single contestant and the test as your contest. Ignore your peers. Before you begin, shut your eyes for just a moment and take a deep breath. As you exhale, imagine all your tension leaving your body.

- Read test directions first.
  Read all the directions carefully. It is so easy to do the wrong thing, or do too much or too little just because the directions have not been read. Take your time with them.

- Skim first.
  Quickly look over the whole test first, then budget your time. A quick skim of the test also allows you to answer a few questions that you feel really comfortable with first; this gives you a boost to tackle harder ones or the ones worth the most marks.

- Watch the clock.
  Know how long you have for the test, and whether extra time will be allowed, then use the time wisely. Break the exam into parts, being sure to do the sections worth the most marks as soon as you have finished a few easy questions first.

Test Writing Tips for Students (*continued*)

- Check as you go.
Occasionally, check the number of the question with the answer you are writing, especially in multiple-choice exams, to be sure they coincide. Also check to see that you are answering the question asked and not something completely different.

- Don't stop.
If you get stuck, leave the question, then come back to it later. Sometimes, something else on the test will help you to remember the answer to the problem question.

- Recall the familiar.
Another strategy for handling the "blank" moments is to pause, take a deep breath, then recall what you *do* remember about the topic or general theme with which you are struggling. Jot down a couple of details you remember about the topic and see whether this jogs your memory.

- Go with the initial response.
If you decide to change an answer during the reviewing stage, but find yourself waffling back and forth between your first response and your second, it is usually better to stick with your first response.

- Do a final check.
Leave time to check your test before you turn it in. Check for missed questions, obvious errors, spelling or grammatical errors, questions not fully answered, directions followed, and finally, your name on the paper.

- Put the test in perspective.
Remember, above all else, that this is just a test—just one moment in your long, full life. It will not make or break you. No matter what happens, you will be OK. If you fail the test, there is always another day. Don't overreact to the importance of any test.

Tips for Students on Organizing Notes and Assignments

- Color-code by subject.
  Use a different colored binder or duotang for each subject to keep things organized. Then, if you have to change classes for a subject, just carry the necessary books for that period. If you are keeping all your books in your desk, it is easy to locate the one you want.

- Date your pages.
  Quickly write dates on the tops of any three-holed pages. Doing this can save lots of time later when you are trying to figure out where a page goes. It is a good idea to date all other work, too, in case you need to know when it was done.

- Use a pocket folder.
  Hole-punched, colored folders that have bottom pockets on each side are great for collecting daily notes for later organization. You just stick the pages in the pockets until you have time to organize them properly.

- Keep notes and assignments in separate parts of your binder.
  Use dividers. It is so easy to shove stuff into the binder and leave it there, but organizing it from the start will save you time. If you are not using binders, you will find it worthwhile to separate all the different subjects by folders.

- Plan to organize your notes.
  Set aside a specific time each week, perhaps 15 minutes on Sunday nights, to organize your notes and make sure they are all in the right place. Take them out of your pocket folders or backpack and put them in the correct binders or folders. Highlight really important points for later quick access.

- Empty the pack.
  On a regular basis—once a week is good—dump out your backpack and throw out what you don't need. If you don't do this, the backpack becomes a monster that eats your notes and pens. The few minutes required to clean it out is time well spent.

- Recycle notes and save.
  At natural term breaks, such as the December break, go through all your binders and folders and take out old material. *Do not throw it away.* Instead, put it in a box and store the box until the end of the year. It's a sure thing that if you throw something out, you'll need it soon.

- Be ready to repair.
  Always carry tape, glue, and three-ring reinforcers with you, so that you can immediately repair torn pages. If you don't, the pages will soon be lost or destroyed.

- Do a check with a partner.
  Every now and again, check your collection of notes and assignments against those of a peer, to see if you have everything important.

- Tap teacher resources.
  Ask your teacher for outlines, study guides, and lists of contents for everything you have covered. These will help you to do a quick check to see if all necessary facts are there.

Tips for Students on How to Be Helped

Teachers want to help you, but they are busy, so you need to use the individual time you have with them wisely. Acting on these tips will help you to do that.

- Ask for help.
Tell your teacher you would like some individual help, and ask for a time to meet. Once established, this is your *tutorial time*.

- Identify the problem.
Before meeting with your teacher, try to figure out exactly what you are having trouble with. Just saying "I can't write" is very vague and will waste time while the teacher tries to narrow down the problem. It's better to say, "I have trouble with getting started" or "Grammar is a problem for me." Naturally, your teacher may already know what you are struggling with, but it's a good idea to recognize it yourself, too.

- List where you want help.
If you want help with several things, make a list and bring it to the tutorial. Doing this will impress your teacher and allow you to get the most out of the time.

- Be on time.
Be at the right place at the right time for your tutorial. By doing so, you show that you are really interested in getting help.

- Bring everything you need.
Come to the tutorial prepared with whatever it is you want help with. For example, bring a pencil and an eraser, as well as the book or problem that you want help with. Don't expect the teacher to pull the material out of the air.

- Be ready to work.
Use the short time you have with the teacher wisely. Focus. Pay attention. Ask questions.

- Ask, ask, ask.
Don't be afraid to ask questions, even if they seem stupid. Your teacher is there to help, and the more questions you ask, the better your teacher will be able to help you.

- Express thanks.
When the tutorial is over, don't forget to thank the teacher for the time.

Questions to Ask About Creating Portfolios

A portfolio is a collection of materials that is usually handed in for evaluation once completed. By looking at it, your teacher will be able to see how you've improved and grown over time. A good portfolio is often quite different from beginning to end. Although all portfolios are different, here are some general questions to ask your teacher. The answers will guide your work.

• What is the purpose of the portfolio?

• What should the finished product look like? Is it to be a duotang? a box? a binder?

• What goes into the portfolio? Do I keep everything related to the topic or just certain items? Is it just for my best work, or for my trials, mistakes, and drafts too? Should I include pictures and charts?

• Could you give me an outline of what the portfolio should contain?

• When do I have to have the portfolio completed? When does it have to be handed in?

• How will my portfolio be evaluated? May I have a copy of the evaluation criteria before I begin?

• Who is the audience for the portfolio?

• How often should I add or remove materials?

• Where will the portfolio be kept? In my desk or locker? Or, is there a special place in the room for portfolios?

• Will the finished portfolio go home with me, or will it be passed on to next year's teacher?

9

Taking Care of Yourself

How often have you heard someone say, "You must take time for yourself"? Teachers are their own worst enemies when it comes to self-time and self-nurturing. The concept of "teacher-free-time" is an oxymoron, unless you work to make it otherwise.

It is important to remember that in the end, you cannot take your students home with you, any more than you can correct all the problems of the world in your classroom. You are human; you have limitations. Think of the teachers you know or have known. How many have left the profession in the first few years due to the overwhelming workload? How many have driven themselves almost to insanity and taken stress leaves? How many really good teachers struggle daily to meet the many professional demands placed on them and have little or no time left for a personal life? So, rather than pushing yourself past your limits, take some well-deserved time now.

This chapter features suggestions for making your room a little more teacher-friendly. Sometimes, classrooms become so cluttered, so busy, so "small," that just walking into one causes a feeling of anxiety. Any ideas that improve upon this situation are valuable. In addition, there are a few tension-causing constants that come with teaching. Dealing with the infamous power struggle is one of these. Even the best teachers have, at some time, had to handle a power struggle. Hints for dealing well with one are included. Similarly, there are tips for managing all the extras, including extracurricular activities, professional development, and peers, in ways that should relieve teacher stress. For it's true that, although you are a nurturer, you frequently do not nurture yourself! And although you already know how to take care of yourself, having some of these strategies written down and visible should increase the chances that you will practise them.

The following poem I composed seems a fitting way to close this section.

I don't want to work today.
Please make those children go away!
I did not get much sleep last night.
Please get those kids out of my sight!
My lessons are not planned, I fear.
Please make the students disappear!

Oh! Here they come. They're here, I see.
Their shining eyes look up at me!
All full of smiles and bubbling noise,
Those darling girls, those precious boys!
Forget those things I prayed before.
I want to teach forever more!

Create a Room You Can Live In

Given how much time you spend in your classroom, it should be both pleasing to the eye and functional. Sometimes, teachers focus so much on making their room *child*-friendly that they overlook their own needs. Don't. Consider the following.

- Establish personal space.

  Your desk should be reserved for you. Tell your students that your desk is your personal space (just as their desks or lockers are theirs), and ask them to respect that. They should not use it for their assignments, belongings, or anything else. Even if your desk is a mess, it will be *your* mess, not theirs.

- Post important papers.

  You need a special place for memos and important papers, so that they don't magically disappear. The best idea for frequently used pages is to tack them to a bulletin board beside your desk. (This works much like the fridge at home.) Don't worry about keeping this board tidy. Tack everything there as it comes to you, and nothing will get lost. You can clean it up weekly.

- Loosen the tight reins.

  You don't have to do it all. Lighten up a little and let some of the need to keep everything in perfect order go. For teachers who absolutely need order, letting the reins slacken may be a tough task, but it's better to spend precious time with children than cleaning your room.

- Delegate the dirty work.

  Others can clean up for you. There are always students who genuinely love to help the teacher, no matter how tedious and nasty the job may seem. Let them tidy the room, arrange "piles," or reorganize clutter. They may not do it exactly as you would, but the day is too short to worry about this.

- Create a clutter corner.

  Get clutter out of sight and it will be less stress provoking. You know what I mean—all the boxes, piles, assortments of "stuff" that invariably work their way into the classroom. Instead of having them lying around, where you can see them and keep thinking that you must do something about them, put them all in one corner and hide them behind a screen. A cardboard screen can be decorated by your students. If it's out of sight, it's out of the stress zone.

- Buy yourself some time.

  Create a silent reading nook. If students who are finished their work have a corner for reading, you will have more time to help the strugglers. No soft couch or chair? Push a table against a wall and throw cushions underneath it and books on top of it. Students, even the big ones, love to crawl under and read.

Defuse the Power Struggle Effortlessly

All teachers, at some point in their careers, are faced with the student who wants to fight. You might have to deal with anything from a temper tantrum in Kindergarten, to a loud argument in Grade 4, to a full-fledged physical fight in Junior High. The following steps generally work well in managing the situation without either of you losing face.

1. Move quickly.
   Move as quickly and quietly as possible to the troubled student.
2. Remind yourself that you are the adult.
   Know that, as the adult, you have the responsibility and the ability to handle this situation so that no one gets hurt, emotionally or physically.
3. Be compassionate.
   Avoid any confrontational comments or non-verbal communications.
4. Remain non-argumentative.
   Do not get into an argument. You will lose.
5. Think quickly.
   Assess the situation. How can you both win and no one lose face? For example, you could calmly and quietly offer the student a way out of the situation. "Take a walk around the school to calm down and I'll return to my desk. We will discuss this here in 20 minutes."
6. Be empathetic.
   Think of how the student is feeling. How would you feel in a similar situation? Don't patronize or offer condescending phrases such as, "I know how you feel." Words like these will just make the student more angry.
7. Remain calm.
   Speak quietly and slowly; keep your voice calm. Don't make any fast actions or speak any un-thought-out words. Maintain eye contact. Keep your face concerned and sincere. Avoid scowling or smiling. Think neutral.
8. Defuse the moment.
   Suggest that you will deal with the situation at a later time. Say something like, "We are both too upset to discuss this right now. We'll talk about it later."
9. Explain what you want to happen now.
   As soon as you get the student's attention, say exactly what you want to happen now. For example: "I am going to leave the room to cool down." "I want you to take a walk to the washroom."
10. Return to the issue.
    Be sure to return to the student and the issue later. At this time you will clearly state the problem as you see it, then ask for the student's interpretation. Be empathetic, but firm. Establish consequences, if necessary, and provide the student with alternative measures (e.g., go for a walk) in case the situation becomes volatile again.

Teachers take on too much. In addition to the multitude of tasks associated with the job itself, they volunteer for all kinds of extracurricular activities, social committees, and community endeavors. This is not news to you, for if you are reading this book, you are already doing something "extra." Here is a list of *gentle reminders* about taking care of yourself. Remember, if you don't take care of yourself, you won't be as good a teacher as you want to be.

• Learn to say "No."
Limit your extracurricular activities. Teachers are expected, in some places, *required,* to take on an extracurricular activity. Taking on several means doing a less effective job of each and straining your personal endurance and stamina. Principals understand and respect the need for self-protection, the need to not spread yourself too thin. Do you?

• Have teaching certificate, will travel.
Get away! Seriously, get away from the city or town in which you teach at regular intervals during the year. Even if you go for only a single night, it is worthwhile to gain a true rest. At home you will always be "on"—a teacher 24 hours a day, seven days a week.

• Buy some peace of mind.
Purchase, even with your own money, good books and resources, and relax in the knowledge that you have information and help at your fingertips when you need it. Be watchful for any materials that have photocopiable pages, handy lessons, or really good ideas. Spend the money and keep these for your personal use. The Internet is great, but extremely time consuming to explore. And, you can't take the Internet to bed, or in a car, or on a plane!

• Follow the yellow brick road—and keep doing it.
Exercise, even if you think you don't have time. Make time! Just 15 minutes of exercise a day—a brief, brisk walk—will do wonders for you. If you aren't a "gym" person, find something physical you like to do and do it consistently. Make it a habit. You'll see results instantly—not necessarily in your physical appearance, but in your brain power and disposition.

• Water. Drink it up!
It's the "in" thing to carry a water bottle and drink water, but teachers often don't have time for "in" things. Make time. Bring a water bottle to your classroom and sip frequently. So much evidence supports the need for water that, as an educator, you cannot afford to overlook it. For example, did you know that even mild dehydration can cause a substantial loss in reflex action, memory, and quick thinking? Drink!

• Take one small step for you, one big step for your class.
Reward yourself with personal time. Its effect is long-lasting and your class will benefit. No matter how much marking you have to do, or how many demands there are on your time every evening, take at least 15 minutes just for you. Use it any way you want—a hot bath, a cool drink alone on the deck, a quiet moment in your room. It's amazing what a short "me-break" can do to restore flagging morale and spirits.

Maximize Your Potential—Think "Lifelong Learning"

Personal and professional development are mandatory. As an educator, you have to keep up with the constantly changing curriculum, not the least of which is the fast-paced technology you are expected to integrate into your classroom. School boards allow time for professional development, so use it. And don't forget about the importance of personal development too. Take a class, join a team or group—you have earned the right to enjoy yourself, even on a school night. The following are some suggestions for professional development. They are intended to remind you of places to go and things to do, rather than stand as innovative ideas.

Places to Go

- Attend teacher conferences and conventions.
  You can get some state-of-the-art ideas and look at the latest in materials available.

- Attend in-house professional development days faithfully.
  The longer you have been teaching, the less you will likely learn, but attend these school- or system-provided sessions nevertheless. There is always the chance that some gold nugget of information will be shared. If not, at least you get a chance to connect with peers.

- Visit libraries.
  Assign one afternoon, at least twice a year, to explore a library that you might not usually visit. For example, check out the library from a neighboring school board or teachers' association, or even a public library with which you are not familiar. Just seeing all the wealth of information can be an enlightening experience.

- Check book depositories.
  There is a wealth of information at the book depositories for school boards. If you do not live near one, plan a trip once a year to visit yours. You'll be amazed at how much you can learn and you might acquire a few book samples too.

- Join a specialist council.
  These inexpensive assemblies promote in-services. They also provide you with an opportunity to meet with your colleagues and share ideas at informal gatherings, such as teachers' time-outs or coffee parties.

- Visit a colleague from a different school.
  Many principals encourage a half-day visit to the classroom of another teacher for the purpose of idea sharing and peer support.

- Draw upon the expertise of others.

  Department heads, team leaders, and seasoned teachers, as well as other professionals in the community, can frequently offer valuable advice and hints. Ask them for it. They will be pleased that you are expanding your knowledge.

- Get to know great teachers' guides.

  Teachers' guides are filled with wonderful ideas. All the big publishing companies are fighting for your dollar, so they put much time and effort into creating the very best in materials, all of which are summed up in the guides. Even if you are not using the books, purchase a teachers' guide to a series for the exciting suggestions and lesson plans it contains.

- Smile at librarians.

  Make librarians your allies. Solicit their assistance and advice regularly. Often they will research and gather resources for you.

- Have coffee with a book.

  If you are lucky enough to live in a centre where there is a large bookstore, allow yourself a couple of hours to browse. Leave your credit card at home, and only purchase the very best book you see. You can learn a lot just by scanning the vast variety of books available.

- Visit the Web sites of big publishing companies.

  These Web sites provide wonderful descriptions of company products, all of which are constantly being updated. You don't have to buy. As a teacher, you can ask for free samples. Then, if you find something fantastic, you can approach your school to purchase.

- Take an Internet tour.

  You'll find an endless supply of lesson plans and ideas; be careful, however. Searching the net is very time consuming. You might be better to delegate the search for a specific lesson or topic to a reliable student or volunteer. Another caution: Don't expect to use a downloaded lesson as is; you will need to adjust it for your specific objectives and that will take more time.

Listening to the Sound of Music: A Happy Staffroom

Although you probably cannot get along with everyone on staff all the time, it is in your best interests to "live" peacefully with them. Here are staffroom survival tips that have proved useful to other teachers.

- Be the sunshine—smile.
  If you concentrate on smiling at your peers, especially as they arrive in the mornings, they will not only smile back, but will appreciate you for it.

- Do something special for everyone.
  This can be as simple as putting a basket of chocolate eggs on the staff-room table or as ambitious as bringing a casserole for lunch.

- Be positive.
  Avoid the temptation to use the staffroom for whining and complaining. It won't improve the situation and will simply spread your discontent to others.

- Deal with differences calmly.
  If you have a serious difference of opinion with a peer, deal with it in a mature and open manner. Remember that you are an adult and a professional, and that you must work with this person for a long time. Words spoken in anger cannot be taken back.

- Avoid secretive talk about peers.
  If you have something to say, say it openly. Don't talk about another staff member behind his back, no matter how tempting this may be or how trustworthy you believe your confidante is. Schools are like little gossip mills. Word gets around. If you don't want the teacher in question to hear something, don't say it.

- Clean up your mess.
  I can't emphasize this enough. On every staff there is the teacher who doesn't do her dishes, clean up her scraps, etc. This person is notorious and is secretly disliked for the messiness. Don't leave a mess even for a short time. Clean up!

- Express appreciation always.
  Say thank you whenever other staff do little things that help you out. Their actions may be as simple as opening your door in the morning. Showing appreciation takes only a second; the effects will be far reaching.

- Respect others' privacy.
  Don't "borrow" things from other teachers' rooms when they are not there or go into their private spaces (desks). This advice applies to the secretary's desk too. Think how you would feel if someone took things from you.

• Be a peer protector.
Never speak badly of any of your peers in front of the students. Even when students come to you with complaints about another teacher, say something neutral such as, "I can't discuss the other teacher with you. Why don't you approach _____ with your concern?" Direct them to the principal if necessary.

• Express your funny side.
Encourage laughter among your peers. If you can draw a laugh from a staffroom of overworked, overanxious, overtired teachers, you have had a successful day. Some teachers are natural comedians. Others have to work at it. Either way, remember that you are an actor, and go for it.

• Praise your peers.
Tell peers when they have done a good job. You know how infrequently teachers hear "good stuff." You always hear when things are going poorly, but seldom when they are going well. Make it your mission to change this. Be on the lookout for the good things that peers do or the successes they have, and tell them. Little notes in mailboxes or e-mails work well if you have trouble giving face-to-face compliments.

Afterword

How do you teach and keep your sanity? With organization and time management. With the help of simple-to-use resources, such as this book. With care and compassion for both your students and yourself.

Consider the road you have chosen. Teaching is an essential profession. In fact, although you have probably heard otherwise, it is the oldest profession, for without teachers, there would be nothing else. Children would not develop the skills and knowledge necessary for independent living, the confidence to face the world on their own, or the social proficiencies necessary for a successful life. From mother to mentor, teachers shape the world. They are the guardians of the past, the profilers of the present, and the creators of the future.

Yours is the most worthy of pursuits, and, I believe, one of the most difficult. You are a teacher 24 hours of the day, seven days a week. You may often feel as if you are unappreciated, overworked, and underpaid. But think of your power. You have an opportunity to make a difference to the lives of children, and, consequently, to affect all our tomorrows. And think of your satisfactions. You have the chance to witness the "aha" when a student "gets it," to see the wondrous smiles of children every day, to share in and make a significant difference in the lives of young people.

I sincerely hope that the ideas in this book will help you to do this. Use the suggestions to help your class become a cohesive, smoothly functioning unit where learning is paramount, but joy is not overlooked. And remember—you are powerful, but, in the end, you "can't take them home with you." Take some well-deserved time for you, too!

Good luck—and good teaching!

Appendix A: Enjoying Impossible-to-Put-Down Books

Build a stock of your own precious books that will travel with you during your entire teaching career. Although I can't begin to list the vast numbers of excellent children's books, I can share ones that I have collected and used with all ages, from Kindergarten to college, so, if you need a starting place or want to supplement your existing personal library, here is the list.

• *Where the Sidewalk Ends,* by Shel Silverstein (HarperCollins)
This book, a collection of poems, had to be included as a fantastic way to turn students on to poetry and to the delight of storytelling through poetry. People of all ages thrill to the whimsical poems. Any books by this author are worth pursuing.

• *The Velveteen Rabbit,* by Margery Williams (A Platt & Munk ALL ABOARD BOOK)
This tale of a boy's beloved toy rabbit becoming "real" is almost a classic.

• *The Kissing Hand,* by Audrey Penn (Child & Family Press)
In this touching tale, the fear of separation that children experience when leaving their parents for the first time is explored through the eyes of a little raccoon.

• *The Classic Christmas Treasury for Children,* edited by Louise Betts Egan (Courage Books)
Here is a beautifully illustrated collection of some of the most beloved Christmas stories, poems, and carols for children.

• *Rose Meets Mr. Wintergarten,* by Bob Graham (Candlewick Paperback)
Enjoy a beautiful story about overcoming stereotyping and bias through compassion.

• *Take Me Out of the Bathtub and Other Silly Dilly Songs*, by Alan Katz (Margaret K. McElderry Books)
The author has rewritten old favorite songs with new, child-centred, nonsense lyrics.

• *For Laughing Out Loud,* selected by Jack Prelutsky (Alfred A. Knopf)
The hilarious poems featured here are guaranteed to bring out the giggles in everyone.

- *You Are Special*, by Max Lucado (Crossway Books)
Here is a wonderful book that deals with the whole issue of equality. It is beautifully illustrated and written—a real winner as far as I'm concerned.

- *Where the Wild Things Are*, by Maurice Sendak (HarperCollins)
This very popular children's book, complete with amazing illustrations, deals with mischief and imagination.

- *The Stinky Cheese Man & Other Fairly Stupid Tales*, by Jon Scieszka (Viking Press)
A must for your room, this hilarious book, which is illustrated by Lane Smith, provides an interesting and surprising twist on familiar themes and tales. Children love it!

- *How Smudge Came*, by Nan Gregory (Red Deer College Press)
Young children will enjoy this beautifully illustrated Canadian picture book.

- *Courage in the Storm*, by Thomas H. Raddall (Pottersfield Press)
Here is a true story of one woman's courage and determination to survive a cruel winter storm in Nova Scotia.

- *Zoom*, by Istvan Banyai (Horn Book)
Excellent for discussion, this picture book demonstrates an unusual perspective on objects: first, showing them close up; then, zooming away to a distant view.

- *The Paper Bag Princess*, by Robert Munsch (Annick Press)
In this amusing tale of role reversals, a poorly dressed girl saves a prince.

- *The Widow's Broom*, by Chris Van Allsburg (Houghton Mifflin)
A picture book, *The Widow's Broom* features challenging content that will interest both older and younger children.

Appendix B: Reading Books That Turn On Even the Most Reluctant Readers

Busy teachers cannot read all the wonderful young adult literature available in a quest for the perfect pick for a class novel study. Consequently, the following list, although by no means exhaustive, suggests a few novels that I know have been successful with students. These novels can be used with both upper elementary and Junior High students. They are not listed in any specific order; however, as the synopses suggest, some may be more appropriate for your needs than others.

A book of less than 150 pages will be considered *short*; one of 150–200 pages will be considered *average*; novels longer than that will be considered *long*.

Note: In all of these novels there are male protagonists. It seems that although girls will read stories with either female or male protagonists, boys prefer those with male protagonists.

- *Stone Cold*, by Robert Swindells (Puffin Books)
  Genre: Realistic, contemporary fiction
  Protagonists: Two Males—one adult, one adolescent
  Why Students Like It: Of all the novels I have ever used with Junior High students, this one truly "hooked" the most. It is a riveting tale, *gripping and haunting,* as the blurb states, told from two different points of view: those of an ex-military man who feels it is his job to rid London of street people, and of a young man who finds himself, through no fault of his own, on the street. Students can't read it quickly enough. An amazing read. Winner of the Carnegie Medal.
  Reading Level and Length: Easy to read; short
  Grade Levels: Best at Grade 8 or 9, because of the social and moral implications.
  Cross-Curricular Possibilities
    - Social Studies: lots on economic content, class values, unemployment
    - Health: issues centred on growing up, leaving home, self-confidence, loneliness, and trust

• *Freak the Mighty*, by Rodman Philbrick (Scholastic Inc.)

Genre: Realistic, contemporary fiction

Protagonists: Two young adolescent males

Why Students Like It: This touching, poignant story centres on an amazing friendship between a boy who is crippled and another boy whom everyone believed was "brainless." Students identify with the problems that both boys endure while trying to fit in with peers and quickly become involved in their lives. The book's finale brings tears to even the jocks in the class. A most unusual story, fast paced and mesmerizing.

Note: A movie, called *The Mighty*, is based on this novel.

Reading Level and Length: A very easy read; short, readable vocabulary

Grade Levels: 4 to 9

Cross-Curricular Possibilities
- Health: all aspects of peer relationships, friendship, loyalty, and love
- Science: biology, growth and development of organisms
- Social Studies: stereotyping and prejudice

• *The Giver*, by Lois Lowry (Laurel-leaf)

Genre: Science fiction

Protagonists: Two males—one adult, one young boy

Why Students Like It: The setting in this stimulating novel is so alien and unusual that all students quickly become totally involved in it. The whole idea of an alternative reality captures their imaginations and encourages them to read on. They identify with Jonas, the young man who is faced with the enormous task of accepting memories and emotions in a world where these are forbidden and kept under control by medication. Jonas goes from what he believes is a perfect world, where everything is completely controlled, to an alien existence where true pain and pleasure exist. This novel has won six major awards, including The American Library Association Best Book for Young Adults.

Reading Level and Length: A more sophisticated read, since it has many layers of meaning. What students get from this novel depends on their individual levels of thinking and examination. It is longer in length than most young adult novels.

Grade Levels: 5–10

Cross-Curricular Possibilities
- Health: peer relationships, friendship, trust, and loyalty
- Science: futuristic developments and concept of how organisms change
- Social Studies: individualism versus group mentality, cultural changes

• *Invitation to the Game*, by Monica Hughes (A Panda Book)

Genre: Science fiction

Protagonists: 10 adolescents—five girls, five boys

Why Students Like It: With so many protagonists, all readers can find someone with whom to relate. They love the vivid description of a rather bleak and gloomy future world, as well as the fact that the protagonists are allowed, by using their wits and knowledge, to escape this existence and discover a new life. The whole concept of starting over on their own appeals to adolescents.

Reading Level and Length: An easy read; average length

Grade Levels: 6–9

Cross Curricular Possibilities
- Science: many references to use of metals and natural resources, references to biology, effects of pollution, and artificial intelligence
- Social Studies: overpopulation, breakdown and development of cultures, effects of government control, as well as overwhelming unemployment
- Health: personal development, friendship, independence, and learning to deal with adversity

- *Driver's Ed*, by Caroline B. Cooney (Laurel-leaf, a division of Bantam Doubleday)

Genre: Realistic contemporary fiction

Protagonists: One adolescent male, one adolescent female

Why Students Like It: It is very easy for young adult readers to identify with the main characters, average high school kids with annoying siblings and parents with unpredictable reactions. The two characters participate in an act that leads to tragedy. "Set against the backdrop of Christmas, and rich with biblical allusions, the novel has a satisfying conclusion" (Susan Tywoniuk, teacher). Readers also love the sarcastic humor.

Reading Level and Length: An easy read of average length

Grade Levels: 7–10

Cross Curricular Possibilities
- Social Studies: society rules and cultural values and morals, juvenile offenders
- Health: excellent novel for dealing with the issues of guilt, reputations, fair-weather friendships, sibling rivalry, hypocrisy, and forgiveness

- *Don't Worry About Me, I'm Just Crazy*, by Martyn Godfrey (Scholastic)

Genre: Realistic contemporary fiction

Protagonist: Adolescent male

Why Students Like It: Written in first person, this incredibly humorous novel captures all the angst felt by a teenage boy with a crush on a girl to whom he's afraid to speak. Readers readily identify with Roob's problems and laugh out loud at his constant, ridiculous daydreams about the object of his affection. Students relate to the friendship, as well as in-school difficulties, experienced by the protagonist and his best friend, and empathize with the concerns both have with their parents.

Reading Level and Length: A very easy read; short

Grade Levels: 5–9

Cross-Curricular Possibilities
- Social Studies: cultural values
- Health: development, adolescent problems, issues with girlfriends/boyfriends, school problems, and parent expectations

- *Beckoning Lights*, by Monica Hughes (A Panda Book)

Genre: Realistic contemporary fiction

Protagonists: First person from the point of view of a young girl, but with strong supporting males (including her twin brother and a First Nations boy)

Why Students Like It: Young readers identify with the true-to-life problems experienced by the characters, all of whom are in Grade 8. They also love the whole idea of telepathy and of the possibility of aliens visiting Earth. With the vision of strange lights, this tale captures the reader's imagination instantly.

Reading Level and Length: This book is included here primarily because it is an exception-
ally easy read, suitable for special classes where students read well below grade level.
It is high interest, low vocabulary, and short, and has relatively large print.

Grade Levels: Reading level, 4–7; content, 4–9

Cross-Curricular Possibilities
- Science: geology, geography, and UFOs
- Health: friendship, siblings, and prejudice

- *The Wild Children*, by Felice Holman (Puffin Books, Penguin)

First published in 1985, this novel is still in print and remains a favorite with adolescents;
because of its wonderful cross-curricular capabilities, it has been included here.

Genre: Realistic, historical fiction

Protagonist: One boy, but with strong supporting male characters

Why Students Like It: Adolescents are enthralled with this based-on-fact tale that describes,
in vivid detail, the hardships that other children must endure just to survive. Alex, the
main character, is suddenly left homeless, without any idea of what has happened to
his family. Readers readily empathize with him as he faces horror after horror and
struggles to stay alive. Set in Russia, at the time of Lenin, this book is haunting. Young
readers cannot put it down.

Reading Level and Length: An easy read, average length

Grade Levels: 6–9, but usually used at Grade 9, in conjunction with the Social Studies unit
on Russia

Cross-Curricular Possibilities
- Social Studies: a perfect fit with the Russia unit at Grade 9. Also good at other grades
for history, cultural development, industrial revolution, and geography
- Health: peer relationships, trust, dependability of peers, growing up, bereavement,
jealousy, friendship, and loyalty

- *The Arm of the Swordfish*, by Madeline L'Engle (Laurel-leaf)

Genre: Realistic contemporary fiction

Protagonist: Adolescent male

Why Students Like It: This exciting book by a famous author deals with the universal
theme of good versus evil, always an interesting theme for adolescent readers. Teenaged boys will identify with Adam's trials, confusions, joys, and issues with trust in
relation to a teenaged girl. Girls will admire the main character and relate to the thrill-
ing situations in which he finds himself.

Reading Level and Length: An average read, average length

Grade Levels: 6–9

Cross-Curricular Possibilities
- Science: marine biology, since that is what Adam is studying
- Health: relationships and development of feelings

• *The Illustrated Man*, by Ray Bradbury (Bantam Books)

This book is actually a collection of short stories. Since I have never found a young adult who did not love the stories, it has been included here. The entire book follows the theme of a tattooed man, whose tattoos come to life when observed, each one telling a different tale. Students love this idea and are readily turned on to the creative and imaginative tales.

Each short story deals with some weakness in society, as well as a moral and ethical issue.

My favorite story in the collection is "The Veldt" so it is detailed here.

Genre: Science fiction

Protagonists: One girl and one boy (brother and sister)

Why Students Like It: Readers delight in the wonderful, futuristic home of the protagonists and marvel at the capabilities of the nursery, which can become anything the children wish it to be. The visual imagery is amazing, and readers quickly become hooked by the sheer nastiness of the main characters. The story is a good example of narration in which the protagonists are not "the good guys."

Reading Level and Length: A fairly difficult-to-read short story, but manageable with some teacher assistance

Grade Levels: 7–9

Cross-Curricular Possibilities

- Social Studies: values and cultural developments
- Science: artificial intelligence, computer controlled living, homes of the future and people's overdependence on technology
- Health: respect, sibling rivalry, parents, responsibility, trust, and honesty

Index